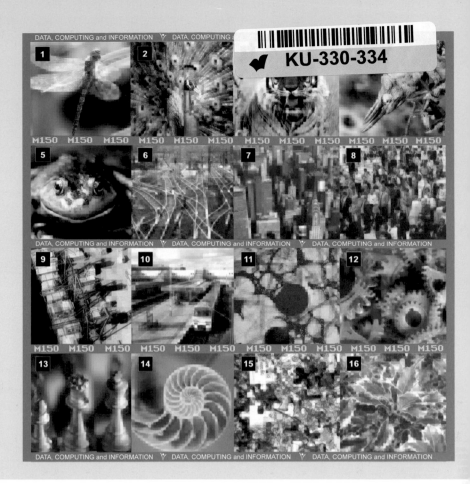

M150

DATA, COMPUTING and INFORMATION

15 Too many secrets?

This publication forms part of an Open University course M150 *Data, Computing and Information*. Details of this and other Open University courses can be obtained from the Student Registration and Enquiry Service, The Open University, PO Box 197, Milton Keynes MK7 6BJ, United Kingdom: tel. +44 (0)845 300 60 90, email general-enquiries@open.ac.uk

Alternatively, you may visit the Open University website at http://www.open.ac.uk where you can learn more about the wide range of courses and packs offered at all levels by The Open University.

To purchase a selection of Open University course materials visit http://www.ouw.co.uk, or contact Open University Worldwide, Walton Hall, Milton Keynes MK7 6AA, United Kingdom for a brochure. tel. +44 (0)1908 858793; fax +44 (0)1908 858787; email ouw-customer-services@open.ac.uk

The Open University
Walton Hall, Milton Keynes
MK7 6AA

First published 2003. Second edition 2008.

Edited and designed by The Open University.

Typeset by The Open University.

Printed in Malta by Gutenberg Press Limited.

ISBN 978 07492 2960 3

2.1

CONTENTS

This unit was prepared for the course team by Mike Richards and Laurie Keller.

1 Introduction

Much of this course discusses issues raised by modern technologies: in particular computing and networking technologies. This unit differs slightly from the others in that it discusses some of the *effects* of these technologies from the points of view of law and social norms.

At present, we are only beginning to realise the power of these new technologies and are scrambling to catch up with their potential – for good and for evil. We hope you will consider any future discussions of technology in this wider context. Although such developments are exciting and may leave us in a daze, it is important that we consider the effects they will have.

This unit draws on a range of real-life examples to show how electronic technologies affect society. We have deliberately chosen examples that affect people's everyday lives. You may have already experienced some of these; you will almost certainly do so in the future.

We have chosen to look at the consequences of computing and networking technologies from two points of view:

1 how they affect privacy;

2 how they affect the ownership of information in the form of intellectual property rights.

This unit discusses some *illegal* activities, but only to illustrate points made in this and other units. The Open University does not condone these activities and cannot be held responsible for any such actions.

1.1 The role of law

Most of us are called upon to make decisions about our own behaviour and the behaviour of others all the time. Increasingly this involves the use or abuse of computing and networking technologies. Once we become involved in the application of a technology we become subject to laws governing those applications. For example, we might be a user of some computer-based service, or we might be the subject of a collection of personal data such as when applying for a passport, opening a bank account or filling in a tax return. We hear stories about such personal data being lost on the news or read about the implications of new technologies in our newspapers. We also, sometimes, write to our MPs or vote based on our views about how new networking or computer technologies are, or could be, applied by governments, organisations and even individuals. The whole discussion of this aspect of the application of technology involves a number of interacting areas of human concern: ethics, moral principles, politics, political systems and law. Ethics and moral principles will be discussed at greater length in Unit 16; this unit is concerned primarily with the political and legal aspects of technology.

Before proceeding further, let's examine briefly the inter-relationship of moral principles, ethics, politics and law. **Ethics** relates to the treatment of questions of right and wrong, based on a set of **principles** of morality (here the term 'principle' means a fundamental truth used as the basis for reasoning about something). Virtually everyone has such a set of principles: ideas about what constitutes right or wrong. For most people, these principles arise out of social conditioning in their childhood, and this conditioning could in turn be based on religious beliefs and/or life practices. Since political systems also arise from the same source, political systems are also based on principles. Because political systems regulate the way large groups of people behave (e.g. by enacting and enforcing laws and by having a major influence on educational systems), these systems also in turn affect a society's underlying understanding of its basic moral principles.

Between different societies or within multicultural societies, moral principles differ. For example, the balance between the rights of an individual person and those of a group differs between cultures, and even within cultures at different times. In some cultures, an individual's 'right' to free speech, the legal protection granted to the public expression of personal views, generally outweighs the right of the stability of the group. This has traditionally been associated with Western liberal democracies such as those in Western Europe and the United States. Other societies have developed cultures in which personal expression is suppressed in favour of stability. Examples of such societies are some cults or religions, totalitarian dictatorships and the communist regimes of the Former Soviet Bloc and the People's Republic of China.

In most societies, the legal system supports the predominant moral principles. However, even within a single culture there are tensions between different moral principles, and these may be reflected in the culture's legal system. For example, in a democracy should the principle of 'free speech' be absolute (anyone can say anything), or should there be limits? Even in Western democracies some things are considered to be so socially disruptive – for example racist views, calls for the violent overthrow of authority, or information on the construction of certain types of weapons – that their publication and promulgation is illegal.

Example 1.1   What the law says you can say

If you think that Western democracies take a uniform view on what one can legally say (this usually means 'publish'), you'd be wrong. In the United States, the First Amendment to the US Constitution guarantees a 'right of free speech' that courts have interpreted to mean that one's right to publish views such as: 'kill all Philodenians' (a mythical group of people) is upheld by law.

A person only steps over the boundary when a *specific* threat is aimed at a *specific person* or *group of persons*, so that saying *'Meet next Thursday outside the Philodenian Social Club and kill the Philodenians'* is *not* protected by First Amendment rights.

In the UK, on the other hand, Part III of the Public Order Act (1986) recognises the crime of incitement to racial hatred. It takes a broader view of what is illegal, and publishing 'kill all Philodenians' is a criminal offence (or would be, if Philodenians were an identifiable racial group). With the Racial and Religious Hatred Act (2006), this was extended to include the crime of incitement to religious hatred. That is, it is now an offence in the UK to incite hatred against a person on the grounds of their religion.

In Germany and France there are even more specific laws prohibiting the publication of material deemed offensive or potentially disruptive, including in Germany what is termed *holocaust denial*.

All these countries are liberal Western democracies, but they take a range of views, mirrored in their legislation, on an individual's right to express views that others find abhorrent.

Formal law is not the only one people recognise. In every society there exists a body of 'law', unwritten and not enforced through the police or courts, that most people adhere to because the penalty for non-adherence is usually social ostracism. This sort of 'law' is referred to as customary law: rules of behaviour set by custom and enforced by social sanctions.

Example 1.2   Free speech and the internet

Early users of the internet viewed it as a forum where anything could be said. Anyone who disagreed with a particular view was expected to mount a defence using the same medium. This led to 'flaming' (as described in Unit 2) in which proponents of opposing views argued with each other vigorously and others joined in on one side or another. The general attitude reflected Harry Truman's dictum: 'If you can't stand the heat, get out of the kitchen!'. As use of the internet spread to a wider, and more international, public, the user community began to feel that the entirely free exchange of views was in some ways harmful. Netiquette grew out of this feeling. Further, governments began seeking to regulate websites which contained material that would be illegal in other media (such as child pornography).

> Netiquette was described in Unit 2. It provides guidelines for electronic communication such as email and bulletin boards.

It is now quite common that public internet forums are being moderated to reduce the risk that the owner of the forum may be held liable for offensive or otherwise unacceptable opinions voiced in the forum. For example, in 2003, NATO Secretary General Lord Robertson sued the owners of the Sunday Herald newspaper over allegations that had been published on the paper's internet message board.

Initially, proponents of the 'free speech' view argued that *anything* should be publishable via the internet, international in its reach and therefore transcending any one jurisdiction or the principles of any one group. They have largely lost this argument to the majority of internet users who want some form of regulation of certain types of content, particularly where that content is viewed as socially disruptive or morally offensive. However, the tensions between free speech and the need for regulation remain.

In this unit, we consider laws that apply to the technologies discussed in this course, though we will not study these laws in great detail. These laws often differ between different countries; within the UK, English law applies in England and Wales, but not Scotland which has its own legal system. However, the situation becomes even more complicated because the UK is also a member of the European Union and must apply European legislation. The UK is also a signatory to a large number of international treaties and agreements which have the force of law. Because many internet-related activities cross international boundaries (for example, an internet user may access a discussion forum hosted in a different country), it can sometimes be difficult to decide which legal regime applies (see the discussion in Example 1.1).

ACTIVITY 1.1

A great deal of legislation deals with issues relating to privacy. This activity helps you prepare for the next section which discusses some aspects of privacy. The activity asks you to complete a questionnaire concerning your feelings about some of the issues surrounding privacy.

2 How private is private?

In modern Western cultures, the notion of *privacy* is central to our way of thinking. In this section you will study privacy, and the ways in which it has been thought about and, in the light of the potential that present-day networking and computing technologies hold for surveillance, how both society at large and you as an individual are affected.

This section aims to:

■ explain privacy and surveillance;

■ show how much information is known about us;

■ show how organisations communicate with us through data and transaction processing.

2.1 Privacy and surveillance

People typically think of privacy in terms of the *separation* of information from public interest: indeed, the *Concise Oxford Dictionary* defines **privacy** as 'keeping some things withdrawn from interest by the public, being undisturbed, or avoiding publicity'. Most organisations concerned with civil liberties base their thinking on that definition. However, Felix Stalder (2002), an expert in the social implications of technology, argues that the concept of privacy is undergoing significant change and arguments for privacy might be better defined in terms of *access to information* and its *fair use*. These categories are based on the relationship between an individual and organisations (whether governmental, quasi-governmental or commercial), rather than on the notion of separation between public and private spheres.

The flip side of privacy is **surveillance**. For most of us, the word conjures up the nightmare world of George Orwell's novel *1984*, in which an all-powerful state spies relentlessly on its citizens and uses the information it gains to enforce conformity. Indeed, the term *surveillance* implies not merely observing someone, but doing so *in order to influence, manage or control their behaviour*.

Orwell and the sociologist Max Weber (who theorised about the technical efficiency and rational superiority of bureaucracy) together conceived one major theory of surveillance which has become known as 'Big Brother'. This is perhaps the type of surveillance we first think of – surveillance by a monolithic, ruthlessly efficient state of its citizens in order to control an individual's behaviour. However, it is useful to recognise two other theories of surveillance.

The first of these is Michel Foucault's notion of the *panopticon*, again based on a notion of surveillance as centrally controlled and coordinated, but not necessarily as a function of the state bureaucracy. Where Weber and Orwell saw surveillance as an imposed and coercive adjunct to policing, Foucault contends that it means that the observed actually police themselves.

The panopticon: a theory of modern surveillance

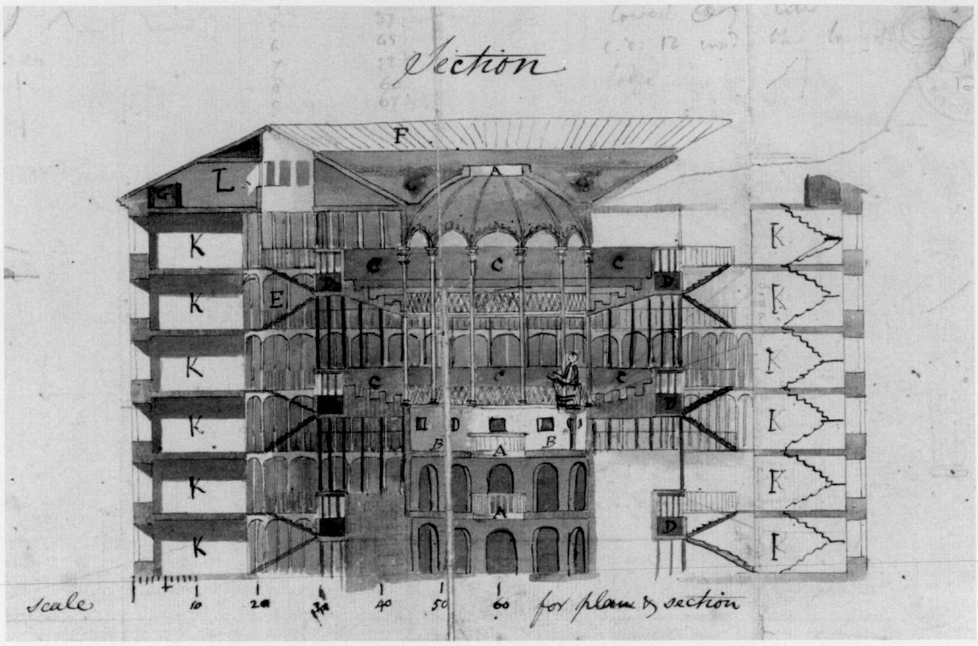

Figure 2.1   The architecture of the panopticon: the observer occupies the central position, from which he or she is invisible to the inmates, who are individually housed in cells around the periphery, isolated from one another by thick, soundproof walls. The other walls and the ceiling of the cell are made of glass

The concept of the panopticon was created by the utilitarian philosopher Jeremy Bentham (1748–1832) as a model prison. Each inmate is kept separate from every other, and the arrangement of the cells or rooms is such that a single supervisor can see into any room at any time. The inmate does not know, at any particular instant, whether or not he or she is under surveillance. In Bentham's view, this would then require the inmate constantly to behave as though he or she were being observed. This approach dictated the design of many nineteenth century prisons such as Pentonville in London and Eastern State Penitentiary in Baltimore which are distinguished by long, straight wings radiating from a central observation tower. The panopticon approach was also used to design several nineteenth century hospitals, allowing doctors and nurses to constantly monitor every patient. A few factories were also inspired by the panopticon, again with the intention that the workers could constantly be monitored by their supervisors; unsurprisingly, these 'factories' were unpopular and unpleasant places to work and soon fell into disuse.

> [T]he more constantly the persons to be inspected are under the eyes of the persons who should inspect them, the more perfectly will the purpose X of the establishment have been attained. Ideal perfection, if that were the object, would require that each person should actually be in that predicament, during every instant of time. This being impossible, the next thing to be wished for is, that, at every instant, seeing reason to believe as much, and not being able to satisfy himself to the contrary, he should conceive himself to be so.
>
> (Bentham, 1787, pp. 29–95)

Thomas Wright (1998) characterises Michel Foucault's *panopticism* as:

■ embedded, or pervasively present, surveillance (every action is visible and potentially observed);

■ asymmetric: the observer can see the observed individual; the observed individual cannot see the observer (so the observer has a form of power over the observed);

■ the observed individual is isolated, physically or socially, from other observed individuals;

■ surveillance is automatic and ubiquitous.

Furthermore, the panopticon concept embodies:

■ a self-policing system in which the individual does not know from one moment to the next whether he or she is being observed, and therefore the individual must constantly comply because, if he or she slips for a moment, that may be the moment in which he or she is judged;

■ an impersonal system which depends on the classification of individuals as, for example, prisoner, student, patient, worker;

■ a capital, not labour, intensive system.

A prime example of Foucault's panopticism is the CCTV video surveillance used extensively in the UK in public spaces:

■ you know you may be watched but you can't see who is watching you;

■ CCTV is virtually ubiquitous in public places;

■ you may modify your behaviour lest you be observed 'misbehaving';

■ observers are more likely to take an interest in young men and teenage boys dressed in a certain manner, or members of certain ethnic minorities;

■ CCTV is a capital-intensive means of surveillance: the UK government spent £250 million installing public-space CCTV systems between 1992 and 2002; in the years between 1994 and 1997 this expenditure represented 78 per cent of the Home Office crime prevention budget (McCahill and Norris, 2002, p. 2).

Studies indicate that CCTV may not be as influential in lowering crime as is sometimes imagined. It may merely displace crime (move it to a less-observed area), change it from one type to another, or cause a temporary diminution. There is some evidence that it works best in car parks, but this may be because of other factors that change at the same time CCTV is installed: improved levels of lighting, for instance.

Two French philosophers, Gilles Deleuze and Felix Guatarri (1987), have inspired a more recent theory of surveillance. Rather than the 'Orwellian' system described above, their 'rhizomic surveillance' resembles the creeping roots of a plant, gradually invading every aspect of an individual's life. Rather than being centrally controlled, surveillance is undertaken by a large number of organisations, each responsible for tracking part of an individual's activities. So a supermarket would track that person's shopping habits for its own purposes; whilst that person's bank would be monitoring their financial activities and their ISP would keep a record of their internet activities. Individually, this information is not of much use, but they could be combined into a detailed 'surveillant assemblage' of a real person.

There are many examples of these new electronic forms of surveillance. It is enabled by a computerisation which allows the construction of large databases which can be searched for personal data in an efficient way. It is also enabled by today's high-speed digital communication links which can quickly transfer large volumes of data (including video streams) in a flexible way over large distances. This makes it possible to quickly gather data that is relevant to a particular surveillance activity.

There has been a trend within the UK for the government and private organisations to gather increasing amounts of personal data for anti-fraud, marketing, policing, future political planning and a host of other reasons. An extreme case is that of the proposed British national identity cards which would require more than fifty individual items of personal information. The card has been variously proposed as a solution to illegal immigration, identity theft, benefit fraud, terrorism and as proof of eligibility to vote. It has been beset by financial, political and technological problems. It is entirely possible that the scheme will have been abandoned by the time you read this unit.

In other countries similar tendencies exist, notably in the USA, with an example being the Computer Assisted Passenger Pre-screening System (CAPPS). This is a data-gathering system in place in the American air travel industry, whose main goal is to help reduce the risk of terrorist attacks. Maintained by the US Transportation Security Administration (TSA), its purpose is to construct a list of individuals considered to be a potential risk to airline or passenger safety. The list is used to keep people viewed as potential terrorists from buying plane tickets or boarding planes travelling in the United States, and to mitigate perceived threats.

The ubiquity of low-cost technology such as digital cameras and in particular the cameras built into an increasing number of mobile phones today has enabled a new kind of surveillance, which is not undertaken by the authorities to monitor individuals, but by the individuals themselves. It is sometimes called **sousveillance**, where 'sous' is French for 'underneath', as opposed to 'sur' which means 'on top' (which rather overturns the traditional hierarchical sense of the authorities as 'on top' and the individual as 'underneath'). This provides a counter-balance to the power of the authorities, since it can be used to document abuse and to mobilise the population in opposition to such abuses. In these circumstances it is sometimes called 'inverse surveillance'. A historic example of the early use of sousveillance is the case of Rodney King, an African–American taxi driver who in 1991 was beaten by police officers in Los Angeles, while the incident was witnessed and secretly video-taped by someone from a nearby apartment. More recently, covert footage of government attacks on protestors have made their way on to the internet from countries as diverse as the United States, Burma and Chinese Tibet.

At the other end of the spectrum on the use of sousveillance, there is an increasing number of cases where it has been used by criminals themselves to record their criminal activity, such as violence against individuals and acts of terrorism. In an attempt to control such criminal activity, countries such as France have introduced laws that equate filming of violent crimes with being an accomplice of such crimes. In the UK, there has been no specific legislation but in March 2008, a court in Leeds convicted a teenage girl for 'aiding and abetting' a case of manslaughter. The girl had not taken part in the attack itself, but had recorded it on her mobile phone.

In general, the legal and ethical policies related to sousveillance remain to be explored, although specific aspects of it (such as recording telephone calls by participants of the conversation) are already regulated. The French law has been criticised since it explicitly protects journalists who record violent incidents from prosecution, but does not extend this protection to private citizens; leading to concerns that it may be used to prevent inverse surveillance against abuse by authorities.

It could be argued that all three theories – Big Brother, panopticon and rhizomic – apply, at different levels within society, to the sorts of surveillance to which those who live in the present-day Western world are subject. Particularly since the events of 11 September 2001 governments, especially – but not only – the US Government, have made use of a variety of apparently benign technologies and loosely specified or newly passed laws to trawl through vast amounts of information about both suspect individuals and organisations. The perpetrators of the 11 September attacks were identified and tracked through everything from car rental and mobile telephone records to their personal shopping. It has been reported that following the attacks, the US authorities tried to create a profile of the ethnic tastes and supermarket shopping patterns associated with terrorism by examining the loyalty card records of the perpetrators.

The use of profiling and surveillance to reduce the risk of terrorism remains highly controversial; whether the benefits of such technology outweigh its disadvantages is a continuing matter of debate. The risks include the perceived danger of unfairly targeting certain parts of the population based on religion, ethnicity, nationality or political belief. A serious limitation of mass surveillance for terrorism prevention is the simple fact that terrorists constitute a tiny fraction of the general population of a given country. This means that, in principle, a technology based on mass surveillance that tries to single out the terrorists from the general population will almost inevitably produce a relatively large set of 'false positives' (that is, members of the population that are falsely suspected of being terrorists). This will happen even if the technology itself is fairly reliable, because of the large number of potential surveillance targets. Whether this is only a limitation of such approaches, or whether it constitutes an actual risk for these false positives depends largely on the manner in which the suspects are then investigated, and whether these investigations are subject to the level of public scrutiny that is generally deemed necessary in a civilised state.

EXERCISE 2.1

As an example of a mass surveillance technique, consider the case of an automatic face recognition system used to search for potential terrorists in public places. Assume (for the purpose of this exercise) that such a system works with 99.99% accuracy in the sense that if the system suspects a given person to be a terrorist, the probability that this judgement is correct is 99.99%. Assume that this system is applied to a population base which includes 1 terrorist in 10 million people. How many false positives would we expect on average in the course of correctly identifying one terrorist?

------------------------------- Discussion -------------------------------

We would expect about 1000 false positives for each person who is correctly identified as a terrorist (since 0.01% of 10 million is 1000). It is worth considering that current face recognition systems work at a significantly lower level of accuracy than the one assumed here – usually well below 90%! This has not stopped the deployment of such systems in a number of locations such as at the January 2001 Super Bowl in Tampa, Florida.

2.2 What might be known about us

The storage and use of personal data is controlled in the UK by the Data Protection Act, 1988. You studied the Act, and the protection it offers, in Unit 5.

There are many things about us which, to varying degrees, in the past, were more 'private'. For instance, in a largely cash economy, what one bought or sold would only be known to those who witnessed the sale or, at worst, would be stored on paper records such as bills of sale or invoices. Writing and storing these was laborious. Thus they rarely recorded more than a brief description of the item and its price.

Now we depend upon third parties, whom we may not even be aware of, to record such things: the credit card company, the bank, the seller's company; so the data is collected by, and passes through, many anonymous hands. Any of these organisations will hold considerably more information than was the case in the pre-digital past: a credit card company will record details of your purchases, know the method you use to pay, how much you owe and to whom (including 'loans' made from the credit card itself), and much else about your credit history, including who employs you, what your income is, and so on.

EXERCISE 2.2

(a) **Briefly write down a list of organisations (other than the government) that know of your existence and what they know about you. Limit this to information you believe is stored in electronic form. Only spend five minutes on this exercise.**

(b) **Are you surprised about the extent to which you are 'known' in this way? Or is it much as you expected?**

Discussion

(a) Your list might differ from mine, but mine includes the following.

■ *Two credit card companies*: they know my credit history, bank (as I pay by direct debit), movements (from purchase records), and purchases, prices and purchasing patterns.

■ A *department store* (store card): it knows the same as the credit card companies – but limited to purchases from one department store chain.

■ *Driver and Vehicle Licensing Agency (DVLA)*: it knows my date of birth, when I passed my driving test, current address and about any endorsements for violations of the highway code within the past 10 years; it also knows the make, model, year and number plate of the car I own and whether I own it outright or not.

■ *Employer*: they know my date of birth, education, marital status, age, current address, salary, tax code, tax office, National Insurance number.

■ *Bank*: it knows the balances in all my accounts, banking transactions (including direct debits and standing orders), current address, banking history over the last 23 years, balances owing on any loans from them.

■ *Insurance companies*: as above, plus claims history and, for my home contents insurance, that I possess some items which are separately insured (computing equipment, for instance).

■ *Web shopping sites*: as above, plus records of past purchases, which they examine to see what my preferences are so they can offer specific recommendations or discounts on other items I may be interested in.

■ *Doctor's surgery*: name, gender, marital status, age, address, health history and health records going back over more than 20 years, prescriptions, known allergies.

You may have come up with many more.

(b)   This is as I expected, but I found that it was impossible to list even a portion of the information in just five minutes. You may not really have been aware of just how much information about you is available.

If you don't have a bank account, credit card(s), a vehicle, a driving licence, and so on, your list will be far more limited. However, even this dearth of electronic information 'says' something about you.

EXERCISE 2.3

Do you think any of the items on your list includes surveillance? Think about the definition of surveillance that appears above before answering.

Discussion

You may have answered that none of the items constitute surveillance. But looking at my list, my credit card companies and the department store with which I have an account very probably observe my shopping behaviour. I usually pay off my credit card bills in full every month, and rarely make large purchases. But every time my buying has neared my credit limit, as it did when I had to make some expensive trips on business, my credit card company has written to me extending my credit limit still further. Why? Because credit card companies make their greatest profit when the card user remains in debt: the more debt the better! So by raising my credit limit constantly in this way, they hope to influence me to spend more – preferably more than I can repay each month so that I begin to owe them interest.

This surveillance does have some benefits. Recently I bought a new laptop at an online store. Within minutes of making the transaction my credit card company telephoned me to confirm that I had authorised the transaction. An automated system had noticed the anomalously large amount being requested on the card and that I had not used that retailer before. It had alerted a human operator to make a call to check that this was not a fraudulent use of my credit card.

All of this can be termed *commercial surveillance*.

2.3 Daily business: transactions and agents

Many people are astonished to discover just how powerful a tool data processing is. In roughly the last quarter of the twentieth century, the technical capabilities of data processing have transformed social conditions. There has been an enormous growth in computerised bureaucracies. Daily life is now largely conducted through **transactions**: the brief and frequently remote exchange of data to accomplish some goal such as purchase or sale, transfer of funds, making a booking and so on. Transactions occur both between an individual and commercial organisations such as a bank, airline, car rental company or retailer, and between an individual and government departments. (There are also organisation-to-organisation transactions, which I will not discuss further.) Data and transaction processing form the life-blood of large organisations everywhere; even small and medium-sized enterprises now communicate with their customers through the power of data and transaction processing.

Face-to-face transactions now form a smaller part of our lives than ever before. Perhaps the most significant social change occasioned by the 'transaction-based society' is that we have had to learn to trust faceless, invisible 'others' with whom we interact to obtain assistance, goods and services from government, businesses, the health service, charities – the *agents* described in Unit 11. As an inevitable consequence of these more formalised and remote exchanges, information people once regarded as 'private' now circulates far more freely than it ever did in the past.

This is true in instances such as correspondence using email. You may email friends, colleagues or relatives, but you probably also correspond through email with people you've never met. This tends to be particularly true of Open University students! Yet more than cursory correspondence or 'conversation' will involve a significant amount of trust – at the least that you will not find information you reveal in such a forum appearing tomorrow in your local newspaper!

EXERCISE 2.4

How many of your fellow students on this course have you met face-to-face? By way of contrast, how many have you corresponded with in student forums or one-to-one through email? Have you met or spoken by phone to your tutor, or do you only know him or her through electronic tuition and email?

─────────────── Discussion ───────────────

The chances are that you will know many more of your fellow students as disembodied electronically-mediated persons than you will know face-to-face, even if you regularly attend tutorials. If you attend tutorials you will have met your tutor, but increasingly you are likely only to know this person 'electronically'.

The question that arises in many people's minds when they consider all this information circulating relatively freely is the balance between information and privacy. The balance depends on events: following 11 September 2001, the US Government, for example, trawled electronically, using techniques known as **data mining**, through vast amounts of transactional data held about millions of people: telephone call logs, internet ticket sales, car rental records, credit card records, copies of email messages held by internet service providers (ISPs).

Although it's a matter of opinion whether you feel that reaction was justified or not, the ease of recording electronic communications makes it possible. Under an unscrupulous regime the possibility of abuse of this capability arises.

This use of technologies such as data-mining on transactional data can be considered as an example of the concept of rhizomic surveillance introduced in Section 2.1. In fact, it is hard to distinguish between the use of data-mining technology to profile customer behaviour, and the use of the same technology to profile potential terrorists.

If our ancestors enjoyed some privacy and even anonymity it was because it was too expensive or too much trouble to copy or publish information about them (we will return to this in Section 6). We have lost much of this privacy as an inevitable side-effect of the way technology enables organisations to gather, store, copy and disseminate data about us. Some examples include the following. (You might be able to think of some more.)

- If you use a credit card or withdraw money from an ATM, the details of the transaction – the amount, the time and the location – are all recorded.

In the UK until 2002, electronic copies of the electoral roll with address information for *all* registered voters were for sale. Only in 2003 did it become possible to opt-out of the electronic version and ensure your address is not included in the data sold.

- If you fill in a survey or send for a brochure, you will see a small box on the form that you can tick to ensure that the details you fill in are not made available to organisations other than the one you are corresponding with (the 'opt-out' box). Many market survey forms ask quite detailed personal questions: where we live, what brands we buy, how much money we earn, where we prefer to take holidays, who we insure our car with, and so on. This data is stored, and can be sold to third parties. If you don't tick the opt-out box, you can find yourself on the mailing lists of organisations you have never heard of before – and people who work in these organisations may then have access to very personal information about you.

- Transacting business by phone, email or the web usually involves giving your postcode. The organisation can then determine your address from your name and the postcode.

- If you carry a mobile phone, while switched on it is in constant communication with the base stations informing them of your location. This could be recorded or used in 'real time' to track your movements.

- The loyalty cards issued by retailers are used to generate information about you, as mentioned in Unit 1. Each time your card is swiped, data about the transaction is stored on a database.

- If you connect to the internet, your ISP keeps a record of the time and location of your connection. European ISPs are required to keep records of email subject lines and the URIs of the web pages you have visited for between six months and two years.

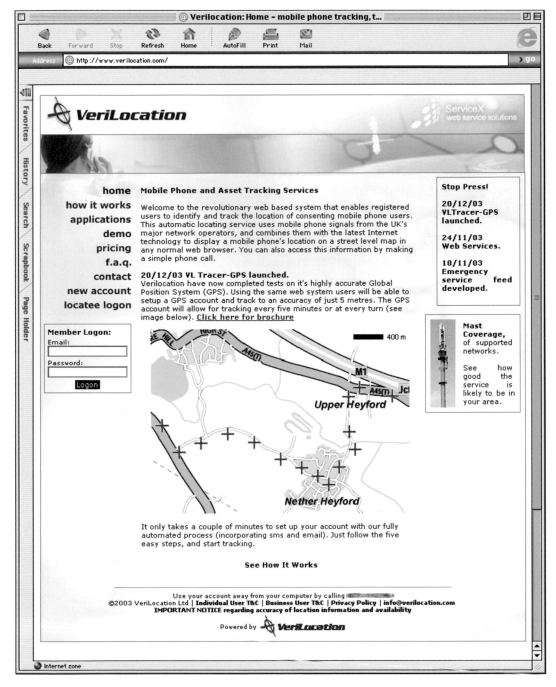

Figure 2.2 Firms such as this will track the whereabouts of any mobile phone, subject to the individual contracting the service proving ownership of the phone and any employee signing a release authorising such tracking. This can be useful for firms with large mobile sales forces or engaged in logistics. But such commercial firms are not subject to the same controls as, say, the police, and the fact that the technology exists means that it is available for misuse as well

M150 CD-ROM

19

■   By combining electronic information from different sources it is possible to apply techniques to trace individuals or build up 'pictures' of groups – the form of surveillance US authorities have used to develop a 'terrorist' profile.

ACTIVITY 2.1

M150 CD-ROM

This activity will help you judge how much information there is about you available on the internet.

2.4 Summary

This section examined the nature of privacy and of surveillance, and the tensions and contradictions that exist between making information publicly available and keeping it private. Examples of the types of information available about each of us were described. The section then examined the technical questions raised by public/private issues: the gathering, storage, uses and access to data. Finally, the section discussed how personal data can be used (and misused) to identify an individual.

3 Invading privacy

You briefly studied spam in Unit 14 from the point of view of security. This section aims to:

- look at spam as an invasion of privacy issue;
- explain how cookies work;
- discuss how even encryption is no guarantee of privacy.

3.1 Spam: invading your email

Spam is 'junk' email (sometimes referred to as **unsolicited commercial email** or **UCE**) that is sent automatically to thousands and thousands of recipients at once. Spam emails started to become a problem with the increasing private use of the internet starting in the mid-1990s. It is currently estimated that more than 80 per cent of all email communicated today is spam. Although one would assume the response rate on this kind of advertisement to be very low, the almost insignificant cost of a single email and the very large set of potential recipients makes the sending of spam profitable for the senders. Once your email address falls into the wrong hands, you are likely to become the target of spam. (Note that if you subscribe to a service that sends email notices of new products or a regular newsletter, whether or not these emails irritate you, they are not spam. You have, whether or not you realise it, solicited them by subscribing to the service. Most such services operate some form of **privacy policy**: it pays to read this before agreeing to subscribe.)

> ## How did spam get its name?
>
> Spam was originally a brand of tinned spiced, chopped ham.
>
> Then it became the subject of a comedy sketch from the television series *Monty Python's Flying Circus*, which was set in a café where every dish on the menu featured spam whether or not the customer wanted spam.
>
> It's that 'whether or not the customer wants it' that is the genesis of the term *spam* in our current context.

Transcription of the Spam sketch

Many of us receive unsolicited mail through the post, and put it straight into the bin. Why is spam any more of a problem than unsolicited mail?

What is marketed using spam? According to one website, the most common uses of spam are for:

- chain letters;

- pyramid selling schemes (in many jurisdictions these are illegal);

- schemes purporting to make money quickly (including fraudulent ones such as the Nigerian 419 scam);

- so-called low-cost loans or other forms of credit;

- advertisements for phone sex lines and pornographic websites;

- offers of software for collecting email addresses and sending spam, and for bulk services for sending spam;

- offering shares in unknown start-up corporations;

- health products and remedies;

- illegally pirated software.

Some people may be upset by some of the spam they receive – distressed that they receive advertisements for pornographic websites, or concerned that their children are receiving such spam advertisements.

What spam can cost

Spam is a cheap way to reach thousands of potential customers. Anyone with a PC and modem can send hundreds of thousands of messages an hour. Increasingly, spam is also sent via so-called 'zombie networks' of PCs in homes and offices that have been infected with malicious software devoted to pumping out millions of spam messages every day. The spammer does not have to pay the connection costs or for the computers. Instead, the cost of spam is born by other internet users.

The internet service provider

Anti-spam websites

To an internet service provider, spam increases the workload on mail servers, delaying *all* the mail waiting to be sent or received. ISPs can use **spam filters** (software to eliminate obvious spam) before it reaches end users, but these filters consume valuable resources. Many ISPs do not use any form of spam filter, forcing the user to deal with the messages.

A second problem for ISPs is that the charge for connecting their customers to the rest of the internet is based on an estimate of the usage by their customers; the larger the number of customers, or the more data they consume, the greater the bill. For most small- to mid-sized ISPs, this charge requires much of their budget. Where spam is a problem, the ISP must choose either to leave its customers to cope with slower internet access or else buy greater capacity, raise its prices accordingly and thus pass the higher charge on to its users.

The recipient

The majority of recipients don't want to receive spam. As a result, spammers trick the recipient into opening their messages. Common tricks are to:

■ make the subject line look as if it is not an advertisement or else ensure the subject line does not trigger a spam filter (common ways are to put spaces between each letter, use a familiar greeting such as 'Hi!' or use the recipient's name, as in 'Especially for you, John');

■ disguise the origin of messages, for example by relaying them through the mail server of an innocent third party (frequently this results in a flood of complaints to the innocent party), or forge the headers of messages, making it appear as though the message originated elsewhere;

■ impersonate messages sent by a reputable company such as a bank, eBay or PayPal. These messages are frequently used by scammers (see Unit 14) in an attempt to trick people into sending personal financial information to criminals.

Email is increasingly vital to organisations that depend on it to conduct business without expensive meetings, phone calls and paper. Individuals may depend on it to aid study (as you are), maintain links to family and friends, and engage in everyday activities. Spam can overwhelm a recipient's electronic mail box. Spam risks compromising the effectiveness of email as a communication tool.

EXERCISE 3.1

(a) If you have an email account other than the FirstClass account provided to you as a student of the Open University, check your inbox to see whether you are receiving spam messages or not. If you are, can you estimate what proportion of your total email is spam?

(b) What do you do when you receive spam?
   ■ **Ignore it?**

   ■ **Delete it?**

   ■ **Follow instructions in the email to be removed from the mailing list?**

   ■ **Use the filtering functions of your email program to send potential spam messages straight to the recycle bin?**

   ■ **Use a so-called spam killer to delete spam on your mail server before it is downloaded?**

Discussion

About 70 per cent of messages received by my private email account these days is spam. My work account also fills with spam, though the proportion is closer to 30 per cent, probably only because of the large volume of messages from colleagues! At work, I use the filtering function of my email program to send suspect spam to the recycle bin, though of course I must check each time to ensure that *only* junk email has gone to the recycle bin. I set up my filters based mostly on phrases in subject lines, such as 'XXX', 'loan', 'credit card', and so on. So I always must check, because a colleague could email me asking for the loan of a book, for example. My system isn't foolproof.

Ignored spam will eventually fill all the space available to your inbox, so legitimate messages to you won't be delivered. Deleting spam as it arrives helps, but it takes time. Also, if you don't check your email regularly junk email can fill your inbox. I resent paying for connection time to receive email that I don't want. There is no easy way to sort wanted email from spam *before* I connect to my account and collect email.

Some people advise you not to respond to a spam message that gives instructions for being removed from the mailing list. Some spammers use this device to update their lists: a response means that there is an email reader at that address! In other cases, the 'remove' instructions are legitimate and you will find yourself removed from the mailing list.

Because of all the problems associated with receiving spam, or trying to detect it automatically, it is advisable to try to reduce the potential for spam by not letting your email address fall into the hands of potential spammers in the first place. Since email addresses can be harvested by programs that search web pages looking for the @ symbol, it is advisable not to display email addresses on web pages in a machine-readable format. Instead, email addresses can be displayed as graphics, or by writing them out avoiding the tell-tale @ symbol, such as 'Bob AT coffeeshop DOT big DOT edu'.

Note that this also concerns email addresses contained in machine-readable documents published on the web, such as Word or Acrobat documents. It is quite instructive to search for one's own email address on the web using a search engine to find out where it is exposed (sometimes in unforeseen places). Although of course the spammers will not search for a specific email address (because if it is already known to them, they don't have to search for it), they may harvest email addresses on the web by searching for fragments of email addresses that may be easy to guess (such as @open.ac.uk as a website www.open.ac.uk exists).

Another potential strategy is to have two different email addresses, one of which is only given to people that can be trusted not to leak it to spammers (such as one's personal friends), and to use the other only for non-urgent or non-important purposes (such as signing up on web pages), so that one does not need to bother checking it on such a regular basis. (Presumably resigning oneself to having to read through mountains of spam to find the useful messages.)

SAQ 3.1

Identify the main costs of spam and give two reasons why it is rarely dealt with effectively.

Answer to SAQ 3.1

The main costs are: connection time to download the email; increased internet traffic on ISPs that effectively reduce their capacity to provide the services that they offer; costs of filtering out the spam. Spam is rarely dealt with effectively because smaller ISPs cannot afford to go to law, and cannot afford to provide filtering services.

ACTIVITY 3.1

This activity asks you to find out what your fellow students and friends think about spam.

M150 CD-ROM

3.2 Cookies: not necessarily a treat

Cookies are short text files exchanged between a web server and client program, designed to permit the customisation of web information. For example, cookies store lists of items a user has selected while browsing through a virtual shop in a virtual shopping trolley.

Cookies are based on a two-stage process.

1   The cookie is generated by a web server, included in HTML information sent to the client program (usually the browser), and stored in the user's computer.

2   When the user directs the browser to display a certain page from the server, the browser will, without the user knowing, transmit a copy of the cookie containing the personal information to the web server, which then uses it.

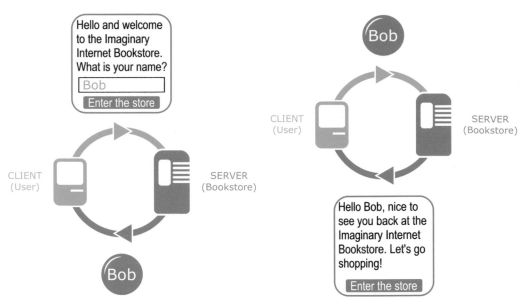

(a)   The process starts when 'Bob' gives his name during his first visit. The web server sends the cookie with Bob's name back to his computer, where it is kept

(b)   When 'Bob' next visits the website, the web server asks Bob's browser for the cookie. When it gets this back, it can place his name in the greeting message

Figure 3.1   The exchange of cookies. When Bob visits the website again, the web server can 'greet' him as though he were an old friend

---

Example 3.1

A user of a customisable search engine selects categories of interest from the search engine's web page. The web server then creates a cookie – a tagged string of text – containing the user's preferences, and it transmits this cookie to the user's computer. The user's browser, if set up appropriately, receives the cookie and stores it in a special file called a *cookie list*. This happens without any notification to the user. As a result, personal information (in this case the user's category preferences) is formatted by the web server, transmitted, and saved by the user's computer.

EXERCISE 3.2

Use the search facilities to look for a file called cookies.txt on your PC and open it using a text editor (such as Notepad on a Windows-based PC). Make sure you include system folders and hidden files and folders in the search. If you have been browsing the web, you will probably find a cookie from DoubleClick.net, Focalink, Globaltrack or ADSmart. It is unlikely that you have ever visited these companies' websites. So why do you have a cookie from them?

Discussion

These companies are tracking your browsing activities so that you can be presented with 'appropriate' advertising. The cookies keep track of the URIs of sites you have visited, the length of time you spend on each site and whether you are a repeat visitor to sites. When you visit another partner site, the information in the cookie is read by the server which selects adverts that are most likely to appeal to your tastes.

By default, the exchange of cookies is done without a user's knowledge. Note, however, that cookies are only passive data files and not programs that can be executed, so they cannot harm your computer or actively pass on private information to third parties. Some people may not be especially bothered by the use of personal information garnered from cookies, but to others this may represent an invasion of privacy. Certainly one potential outcome is that the hapless user receives personally addressed unsolicited commercial emails!

Recent versions of browsers allow you to check which cookies you have (and set expiry times or delete those that are unwanted), reject cookies or issue a warning message when a website tries to send a cookie. In Internet Explorer this appears under the Tools / Internet Options menu at the Privacy tab and is based on what to do 'When receiving cookies'. It allows the user to select from a range of pre-defined privacy requirements levels between the following two extremes (and also allows advanced users to define their own policies):

- accept all cookies offered, without warning;
- never accept cookies.

Firefox is similar. Select the Edit / Preferences menu (and then the 'privacy' tab). Firefox enables the user to:

- disable cookies;
- enable or disable cookies from specified websites only (for example one can specify that cookies from companies like DoubleClick are rejected);
- specify when cookies should be deleted;
- enable all cookies.

Both browsers allow you to manage your cookie file.

Are cookies all bad?

Cookies were designed as a simple mechanism to make it easier for users to access websites without having to go through a lengthy process of identifying themselves every time they repeat a visit. On a first visit to a given site, a user may be asked for a name and perhaps a password or some personal information to gain access to that site again in the future. The site then creates a cookie containing this information, stores it on the user's system and when the user next returns to the website it will request the cookie to determine who you are and whether you have authorisation. A site will only have information that you have entered, so if you use a site frequently, it may be quite reasonable to store a cookie for it.

SAQ 3.2

(a) What was the cookie designed to do, and how can it be misused?

(b) What can a user do about receiving cookies?

Answer to SAQ 3.2

(a)   Cookies were designed to allow the personalisation of information, for example through search engines, by recording preferences stated by the user. They can be misused to gather information for direct marketing.

(b)   A user can set browser preferences to filter or reject cookies or can use browser facilities to manage the cookie list.

Behind the scenes: data flows

'Data flow' refers to the gathering of information from different sources, combining, manipulating and (often) passing it on to others, usually in the interests of commercial activities. The term also has a different, but related, technical meaning.

Much of the data flow activity related to processing user data gathered on the internet begins when online companies obtain names and email addresses of people who visit their websites and choose to open an account or opt to receive further information by post or email. This is then associated with a cookie that records various activities that the user carries out online during that and subsequent sessions. DoubleClick's website, for example, offers the following services to its customers:

■   analysis of how recently visits have been; how frequently the site is visited and the monetary value of sales to different *customer segments*;

■   which segments of visitors become customers and which segments of customers become repeat customers;

■   demographic information about website visitors (such as whether they are located near to or far from a retail shop, their geographic location, and whether they are web surfing at work or at home).

By expanding this capability with technologies such as spyware, chat-room analysis and data garnered from an individual's transactions with databases, it becomes possible to follow an individual's email and keyboard activities. This may be supplemented by purchasing information from 'off-web' firms and linking that information together with their own information.

Companies vary in their attitudes to this powerful cluster of technologies. An extreme response was that of Sun Microsystem's chief executive, Scott McNealy in February 1999 when it was pointed out to him that one of his company's products could enable someone to track the product's user's movements: 'You have zero privacy anyway. Get over it.' A more typical response is to agree that the goal of protecting personal information is important, but to argue that legally enforceable data privacy rights would be catastrophic to industry.

In March 2008, the three largest ISPs in the UK (British Telecom, Virgin Media and Carphone Warehouse's TalkTalk), which between them account for more than 70% of all broadband users, announced an agreement with a relatively small company known as Phorm. ISPs have been looking to increase their profitability, and one method is by improving the relevance of adverts shown to users when they visit websites in the hope that more people click on a link and visit the advertisers' sites.

Phorm has designed special hardware and software which is installed at the ISPs' sites. When one of the ISP's customers makes a request for a web page, the Phorm system captures the URI of the page, any search terms and enough of the page to allow it to categorise the contents of the page into one of a number of predefined categories. A cookie is placed on the user's computer containing anonymised information about the type of material the user has been requesting. When the user then visits one of Phorm's partner sites belonging to the Open Internet Exchange advertising group, they will see adverts relevant to their browsing habits.

Phorm has proved to be wildly controversial amongst internet users with the vast majority of users expressing alarm that it will infringe their privacy. Phorm itself has tried to reassure users by confirming that it will not capture encrypted data, the contents of webmail pages, credit card and bank account numbers or the IP addresses of individual users. However, even if Phorm is never deployed, it is merely the first of many similar schemes that will soon be introduced by ISPs in Europe and the United States.

Companies have a strong economic motivation to reduce the levels of customer privacy; different users are willing to pay different amounts for the same product. If individuals can be identified, if not by name, then by their spending power, they can be targeted with different prices. A long-standing example can be found in the pricing of international flights. Flights in which the user makes the outward and return legs during weekdays are generally more expensive than those over a weekend for the simple reason that most weekday flights are made by business travellers whose tickets are paid for by their employers.

In 2000, the online bookstore Amazon briefly experimented with a system of differential pricing by which new customers would receive lower prices than established customers. Such were the number of complaints that the trial was abandoned.

It is quite easy to imagine a system that tracks each user's individual activities to build a profile of that person. This profile could then be used by companies to decide on the prices that customer will be offered. A travel agent could see that the customer had just bought a ticket for an expensive industrial conference at the destination and therefore increase the cost of flights for that customer alone. A more chilling possibility is that insurers might be able to see that a customer had been researching information about diseases before applying for medical or health insurance and increase the premiums on that policy.

The European Union has relatively stringent prohibitions against using data for purposes other than those which prompted their gathering in the first place. However, this technology is both powerful and international, and therefore not easily subject to governmental controls; it is perfectly legal for a company outside of the EU to process the personal data of an EU citizen in a manner that would be illegal within the Union. Significantly, in many respects, US law is much weaker than European law about the possession, processing and resale of personal information.

EXERCISE 3.3

(a) **Have you ever read a website, mailing list or other electronic medium's privacy policy?**

(b) **Have you ever tried to look up information about how to protect your own privacy on the web?**

Discussion

(a) Only you can answer this. If you haven't previously done so, consider doing so the next time you look at a website or consider joining a mailing list. Decide whether, on the basis of the privacy policy, you understand what might happen to information about you gathered as a result of your visit or subscription, and whether you feel that this is reasonable.

(b) Again, only you can answer this. There are a number of websites and articles available about this, and as part of studying this course you should consider conducting your own 'privacy audit' to determine what you want to do about what is already known about you and by whom, and whether or not you wish to reveal more about yourself.

An authoritative report into online privacy was produced in 2003 by Joseph Turow, Professor of Communication at the University of Pennsylvania's Annenberg School for Communication; it concluded:

> When consumers are unaware of the data flows that take place behind their screens, they cannot really engage in the kinds of informed cost–benefit analyses that writers ... suggest take place when consumers 'pragmatically' give up information about themselves. What consumers can't evaluate are the costs involved when marketers or governments hitch seemingly trivial information the consumers have allowed them to track, such as TV viewing habits or fashion interests, to other knowledge in order to create powerful profiles about them. Correct or not, the profiles can impact people's lives in ways they can't control for lack of knowledge. Online and offline media might change content

depending on what the media firms and their advertisers 'know' about them. The consumers might receive different ads and different discounts than they had in the past. Government agencies might pay more or less attention to them than to others.

This study found that when adults who use the internet at home are brought face-to-face with a common approach to collecting, interconnecting and using their online information, they overwhelmingly reject it. [H]owever, ... these people don't go out of their way to learn what is going on with their online information. 64 per cent say they have never searched for instructions on how to 'protect information' about themselves on the web. Large percentages of online-at-home adults have little, if any, experience with basic internet privacy tools.

(Turow, 2003, p. 33)

SAQ 3.3

How well do you feel the description of data flows in this section matches with the 'rhizomic' theory of surveillance of Deleuze and Guatarri described in Subsection 2.1?

Answer to SAQ 3.3

It could be said that the 'rhizomic' theory of surveillance encapsulates almost exactly the powerful technologies that aid data gathering and the 'flows' that occur afterwards to build a profile, or persona, of an individual based on streams of data from different sources.

3.3 When should users be able to keep things private?

As explained in Unit 14, it is possible to preserve privacy, even where a network is vulnerable to attack, by using encryption. Business-to-business and sensitive business-to-customer transactions (such as those involving banking, fund transfers and credit cards) benefit from encryption and this is usually provided by means of secure servers (described in Unit 1 and, in the context of security, in Unit 14). People exchanging information they consider private, e.g. through emails, may also want to use encryption. In offering this form of protection, encryption provides benefits. However, encryption could also allow criminals and terrorists to coordinate plans and the execution of their crimes with the same level of protection. Many of us would say that this was a serious disadvantage of encryption.

Thus, there is an obvious conflict between holding personal information (and keeping it private) and releasing it to authorities (especially when crime is involved). This raises a pair of questions; firstly, when should internet users be able to keep their information private? Secondly, given the widespread availability of strong encryption technology to private users (as discussed in Unit 14), it raises the question of whether a government can actually force access to a user's encrypted data.

In this section, we focus on the second of these questions, and in particular on a specific technological solution that had been proposed for it in the past (the so-called Clipper chip).

A novel solution

During the late 1970s and 1980s, strong encryption technology (such as the encryption algorithms RSA and DES discussed in Unit 14) became available to technologically interested individuals, including activists that promoted its use to evade governmental surveillance. By the early 1990s, the United States government recognised that both the pro-encryption and anti-encryption camps had equally valid viewpoints: whilst individuals have a right to privacy and security; the interests of justice may require that law-enforcement organisations are able to read encrypted materials.

The US Government proposed a novel form of encryption which permitted access to the encryption key by a *trusted third party*.

Trusted third parties and key escrow

You may never have heard of the terms **trusted third party** or **escrow agency**, but they are surprisingly common in everyday life. Some examples of trusted third parties that you might have encountered are property rental agencies who hold keys on behalf of the owners and take payment from tenants; judges and juries in courts who are expected to be impartial to both parties in a case; election authorities who count the number of votes and monitor the fairness of an election; and notaries who are responsible for witnessing signatures on documents such as wedding registers and passport.

It has been proposed that trusted third parties could be set up to hold copies of encryption keys. This would be in contrast to the original public–private key method discussed in Unit 14, where the private key always remains under the control of its owner. Crucially, trusted third parties would have copies of *private* keys.

The concept of a trusted third party is *not* the same as a **key server** such as that discussed in the previous unit. Key servers only hold copies of public keys, which *cannot* be used to decrypt encrypted documents nor attached as a digital signature.

Under normal circumstances a private key is only accessible to the holder. However, the key *could* be released to police or intelligence agencies if they needed it for an investigation. The process of handing a key to a trusted third party is known as **key escrow**. The key itself is said to be **in escrow**.

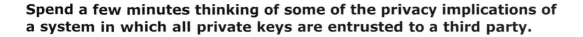

EXERCISE 3.4

Spend a few minutes thinking of some of the privacy implications of a system in which all private keys are entrusted to a third party.

— Discussion —

The third party would have access to the private keys of those who have entrusted it to them. From your studies of Unit 14, you will remember that the private key allows files to be decrypted, documents to be signed, and so on, in the name of its owner. The trust placed in the third party, not to do any of these things, is therefore great.

The Clipper chip

A proposed compromise between personal privacy and the need for intelligence was the **Clipper chip**, a specially designed microprocessor which would be built into telephones, modems and the like. In normal use, it would ensure the privacy of any two parties sending and receiving a message. However, in the event of suspected criminal activities, Clipper provided a method for government agencies to decrypt encrypted messages.

The encryption to be distributed on the Clipper chip contained three pieces of identification:

1. an 80-bit **unit key** unique to each Clipper chip;

2. a **family key** common to all Clipper chips;

3. a unique serial number.

Clipper was a *key escrow encryption system* since copies of the unit keys would be held in escrow. The unit key would be divided into two parts and sent to two escrow agencies: one part to the United States Treasury and the other part to the National Institute of Science and Technology (NIST). In normal use, only the device's user would have access to the full unit key.

EXERCISE 3.5

What is gained by dividing the unit key into two and distributing it to two escrow agencies?

— Discussion —

Security is gained. Just as tearing a treasure map in two means that two people have to cooperate to find the treasure, decryption of Clipper messages would only be possible by recovering the entire key from the two agencies.

When two devices fitted with Clipper chips communicate with one another, they first negotiate an 80-bit **session key** unique to that communication session, i.e. it is a one-time key.

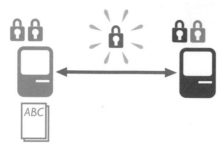

Figure 3.2   The first stage of transmitting information by Clipper. The sender's machine (on the left) and the recipient's machine agree on a shared session key (shown in purple). This diagram also shows that the two machines share a family key (shown in grey), but have their own unique unit keys (in blue and red respectively)

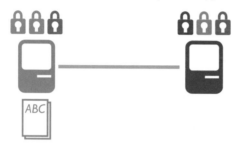

Figure 3.3   A copy of the session key now exists on both computers

The sender's computer now encrypts the message using the session key.

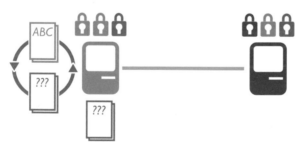

Figure 3.4   The message is encrypted on the sender's computer using the agreed session key

Next, the sender's Clipper chip encrypts the session key with that chip's unit key.

Figure 3.5   The sender's Clipper chip then encrypts the one-time session key using its unique unit key

Some additional information is added to the encrypted session key and the whole encrypted with the family key to create a piece of information known as the *law enforcement access field* (LEAF).

The LEAF is added to allow law enforcement agencies to determine who owns the unit key itself.

Figure 3.6 The encrypted session key is then further encrypted using the family key along with some other information to form the LEAF. The sender's computer is now ready to transmit the encrypted message

The LEAF is then transmitted along with the message itself.

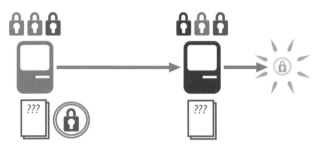

Figure 3.7 The sender's computer now transmits the encrypted message and the LEAF. The encrypted message is received by the distant computer. In normal use the LEAF is discarded

The recipient uses their own copy of the session key to decrypt the message contents.

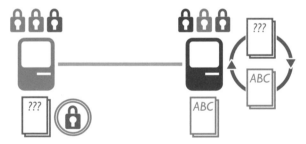

Figure 3.8 The recipient's Clipper chip decrypts the data using its own copy of the session key. The session key is discarded

Clipper was intended to be used in a wide range of domestic communications devices and therefore the entire process of encryption and decryption would appear to be seamless to the user (indeed they might not be aware that they were using an encryption system). It would all happen 'invisibly', neither sender nor recipient being required to do anything.

Access to Clipper encrypted messages

Under normal circumstances the LEAF would simply be discarded – it is of no use to the two participants. However, if an authorised organisation had an eavesdropping device in operation, it would be able to obtain the encrypted message and the LEAF. The LEAF was encrypted using the family key, which is common to all Clipper chips.

Figure 3.9   In eavesdropping, the investigators intercept the encrypted message and a copy of the LEAF

Therefore the agents would be able to use their own copy of the family key to decrypt the LEAF, which contains the session key needed to read the message. But that key would still be encrypted with the sender's unit key.

Figure 3.10   The investigators are able to use their own copy of the family key (shown in grey) to decrypt the LEAF. They would then possess the encrypted session key, but be unable to decrypt it

In order to read the message, the agents would have to obtain copies of the unit key from the escrow agencies. This requires that the agents satisfy a judge that there is a case for releasing the keys. If granted, the two escrow bodies would release their halves of the unit key to the law enforcement agency.

Figure 3.11   Following a judicial order, the two escrow agencies release their halves of the unit key. The unit key is then reassembled on the investigator's computer

The completed unit key is then used to decrypt the session key.

Figure 3.12 The completed unit key is used to decrypt the session key

And the session key in turn can be used to decrypt the entire message.

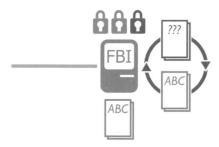

Figure 3.13 Finally, the decrypted session key is used to decrypt the original document

Whatever happened to Clipper?

Despite the direct support of the Clinton administration, Clipper foundered as a result of disapproval from civil rights activists, the computing community, major media organisations (such as *The New York Times*) and Congressional opposition. Public opposition had already made Clipper deeply unpopular before the discovery of a flaw in the Clipper chip; researchers discovered that it was possible to 'crack' Clipper protection without access to the unit key. Its security was an illusion.

Problems with key escrow

Key escrow appears to offer a compromise between individual privacy and the necessity for law enforcement bodies to prevent potentially criminal activities. However, there are three major problems with such systems.

1   Who holds the keys?

    Key escrow relies on copies of all private keys being held by an escrow agency; clearly any trust in such a system depends on how far people will trust the agency. A compulsory key escrow system for the UK was proposed by the British government in 1998 (a year after promising *not* to regulate encryption!). In this system the keys would be held by a government body. However, law enforcement is also usually a government responsibility, so the independence of the escrow agency would have been in some doubt.

    The British key escrow system was withdrawn as a result of concerted academic and industrial pressure – both on the grounds of trust, and also because multinational companies threatened to move away from the UK if they were forced to register encryption keys with the government.

2   How are the keys accessed?

Assuming an escrow agency could be created, the second potential problem lies with the requirements that must be satisfied before the keys are released to the law enforcement agents. Naturally, individuals would want these requirements to be difficult to fulfil. Conversely, law enforcement bodies would prefer a relatively simple process. From a law enforcement point of view, the need to obtain a warrant from a judge might be seen as slowing the process.

3   How secure is the escrow agency?

The escrow agency holds copies of every key in circulation; as such it becomes a target for anyone wishing to abuse the system. The agency must not only be protected from external threats but also from disgruntled or criminal members of staff who could steal keys and misuse them. You may wish to consider some of the examples from Unit 14 and decide if you think private keys can ever be held safely by trusted third parties.

EXERCISE 3.6

Consider the following hypothetical situation.

A fictional government is proposing to introduce a key escrow encryption system that will be fitted to all communication equipment sold in the United Kingdom. Each chip will have a unique 25-bit encryption key. A copy of the key will be deposited with a government-controlled escrow agency. Keys will be released automatically to law-enforcement organisations upon application to the Home Secretary.

Use the information in this unit and in Unit 14 to locate shortcomings in the plan, and propose an improved implementation of the government's proposal.

— — — — — — — — — — — Discussion — — — — — — — — — — —

You may have identified the following:

- the scheme uses extremely weak encryption keys (see Unit 14);
- the government retains control over the escrowed key, which might compromise the scheme;
- keys will automatically be released from escrow when requested.

These problems could be resolved by:

- a longer key length;

- splitting the escrowed key between two respected non-governmental agencies;

- releasing keys only when the need has been proved – to an independent party such as a judge.

SAQ 3.4

(a) How does the key escrow system differ from the ordinary asymmetric key encryption techniques you studied in Unit 14?

(b) What is the major vulnerability of key escrow systems?

Answer to SAQ 3.4

(a) *Private* keys are stored with a trusted third party (the escrow agency).

(b) If the entire key is held by a single agency, anyone able to compromise that agency's security could gain access to private keys.

3.4 Summary

This section examined what broadly might be called invasions of privacy: spam (unsolicited commercial emails) and the hidden exchange of personal information through cookies. This was followed by the examination of the Clipper chip, which would have enabled personal privacy to be maintained through encryption hardware in every communications device, using key escrow as a means of allowing the authorities access when necessary. But a potential technical solution foundered through a combination of some technical weaknesses and worries about misuse of the system.

4 Owning and controlling information

The other side of the coin of privacy is the desire to publish. There are probably as many reasons for publishing information as there are people who want to publish, but the main ones are to:

- make money, for example by selling what one publishes;
- further an interest, such as a hobby, by contributing information;
- advertise one's products or services;
- enhance one's own fame.

The digital era has made the task of writing text or music or creating images (such as those by Christine Martell in Unit 1) or even films easier than ever. These can then be advertised or distributed via the web. (For example, online photo libraries allow purchasers to download a photograph upon payment, though to prevent people from simply copying a photo using, say, screen capture techniques, they are published with a large 'watermark' – described below – on them that identifies them as being obtained illegally.) With the advent of the personal computer small companies specialising in media production have flourished. It is now possible for a relative novice to create, edit and distribute a film or musical composition using a single computer.

However, such developments have also made it easy to steal such materials or to make money by buying up property such as domain names. This section aims to:

- examine the problem of piracy when information is essentially unprotected;
- examine some proposed remedies which use some of the technologies discussed in Unit 14 and earlier in this unit;
- illustrate just how important encryption is to every person – even if they do not use a computer.

4.1   Who owns information anyway?

In this section you will learn a little about the legal protections given to information and ideas. This area of the law is known as **intellectual property**, a huge, complicated and very profitable legal minefield. Fortunately, this is not a law course!

There are three broad areas of intellectual property law, dealing with patents, trade marks and copyright.

Patents

A **patent** is a form of protection given to the creator of a piece of work which gives the creator exclusive rights to produce that work for a limited period of time in exchange for the creator making public the design and workings of the item. If an item is to be patented it must be judged original and not an obvious development of an existing idea. These decisions are made by national or international patent authorities (sometimes called patent offices).

There are differences between countries as to what can be patented; most patents are awarded for industrial processes and machineries, but they have also been awarded for novel plant breeds, genes and business models. One crucial difference between patent regimes is that the United States allows for software to be patented, whereas the UK and the remainder of Europe do not currently permit this.

Trade marks

Companies are normally very jealous of their brand identification: they see this as key to establishing and maintaining a loyal customer base, to building a reputation (for example for quality, value for money, or for leading fashion), and for public recognition. Name-brand advertising began in the nineteenth century in response to widespread adulteration of foodstuffs: companies fought to establish their brand as 'pure'. Since then brand names have been extended to all manner of goods and items including the names of characters in books and movies!

Rights to a brand name or a designating symbol or phrase are established through the so-called **trade mark**, which is a legal term meaning that a name, symbol or phrase is registered as belonging to a particular company and cannot legally be used by any other.

Trade marks have to be registered, renewed and defended in law – if they are not, then the trade mark is deemed to have lapsed and the term can be used by anyone – some examples of former trade marks that we use everyday are petrol, yo-yo, escalator and aspirin. Companies spend large sums registering, enforcing and defending trade marks from competitors. A trade mark is indicated either with the ^{TM} or ® symbol; the latter shows that a trade mark has been registered with a government body and offers additional protection in the event of a legal dispute.

> Alternative names for trade mark are 'mark', 'brand', 'label' or 'logo'.

EXERCISE 4.1

Spend no more than five minutes looking for trade marks on items in your house or office. You will often find details of the mark in the small print of manuals and the slip-covers of DVDs and CDs, or even printed on the bottom of items themselves. Why do you think there are quite so many?

Discussion

I'm always surprised by the number of ^{TM} and ® symbols that can be found on items – especially toys and games based on television programmes or movies.

The reason for their abundance is that the trade mark holder must always defend their mark. If the item appeared without the appropriate symbol it could be considered that the mark is not being actively protected, in which case a rival company may attempt to start using the mark on their own products.

Copyright

The most important of all intellectual property concepts is that of **copyright** which originated in the United Kingdom in the early eighteenth century. Under copyright law, the creator of a piece of work is given the exclusive right to benefit from their work for a period of time, after which the work is made freely available to all. Copyright was designed to benefit all parts of society – the creator would be rewarded for their work by being able to charge for copies in the knowledge that no one else could do likewise, whilst the rest of society would benefit by having access to the work when the copyright period expired.

Copyright can be applied to any intellectual or artistic work that has been realised in some form. A partial list of such works are books, poems, plays, movies, dances, musical scores, audio recordings, paintings, drawings, sculptures, photographs, software, radio and television broadcasts, and industrial designs. Crucially, ideas that have not been realised cannot be copyrighted.

SAQ 4.1

Which of the following can be copyrighted? A comic book, an Open University podcast, an abstract painting, the design of a car.

Answer to SAQ 4.1

They can all be copyrighted.

The copyright symbol – © – is often used by large companies to assert their ownership of materials. It is not necessary to use this symbol to claim copyright over an item, so you cannot assume that an item is not protected by copyright just because the symbol is absent.

The 1710 UK law that created the concept of copyright dictated that works would be protected for 14 years from the date of publication; after which the author could apply for a copyright extension for a further 14 years.

However, in no circumstances could the **copyright term** extend beyond 28 years. Since then, there has been an almost inexorable increase in the length of copyright.

Copyright terms in the United Kingdom are almost uniquely complicated. Rather than adopt a single period of copyright, the Copyright, Designs and Patents Act (1988) lays down a series of copyright terms for different media, depending on the type of media, the date of publication and the country of origin. Broadly, they are as follows:

- for printed materials (such as this course unit), the term is 25 years from the date of publication;

- broadcast material (such as television or radio programmes) created in the UK are protected for 50 years from the date of first broadcast;

- audio materials are copyright for 50 years from the time they were first recorded;

- copyright for the composition of dramatic works such as movies, novels, music, literature, art or plays lasts for 70 years after the death of the author or director. If more than one person was responsible, the 70 year period extends from the time of the death of the last creator.

SAQ 4.2

(a) **Is this course text protected by copyright?**

(b) **When will the copyright expire on the recording of the Beatles' song 'Yellow Submarine' (released in 1966)?**

(c) **When will the copyright expire on the song 'Yellow Submarine' which was written by Paul McCartney and John Lennon?**

(d) **'Bleak House' by Charles Dickens was published in 1853. Is the original text still under copyright?**

Answer to SAQ 4.2

(a) Yes it is. You can find the copyright notice on page 2 of the unit.

(b) Assuming there are no changes to copyright law in the United Kingdom (see the note below), the copyright on the song will expire 50 years after the recording, i.e. 1966 + 50 years = 2016.

(c) It's too early to say. The copyright for the song will last for 70 years from the death of the last surviving author. At the time of writing, Paul McCartney is still alive and well and 'Yellow Submarine' remains firmly under copyright.

(d) No. The text of 'Bleak House' is in the public domain. Even if the current legislation had been in force at the time of Charles Dickens' death in 1870, the text would have entered the public domain 70 years later in 1940. Copyright for new editions of the book will be granted to the publisher and will extend for 25 years from the publication date of the new edition. Significantly, this is a non-exclusive copyright; individuals can continue to access the original text of 'Bleak House' and other publishers may print their own editions of the book (for which they too will be granted copyright).

Unlike patents and trade marks, copyright is an automatic right given to the creator of any suitable material – it is not granted by an outside body. In many cases, anything you create is your copyright; however, if you are contracted to produce material – for instance as part of your job – then copyright is usually transferred to your employer.

EXERCISE 4.2

Why do you think The Open University has the copyright on this unit rather than the author?

Discussion

If the copyright remained with the author, I could take this work (during the production of which the OU has paid my salary) to another publisher who would benefit from the OU's investment.

At the time of writing (early 2008) there was pressure on the UK government and the European Union to extend the copyright term on sound recordings from the current 50 years to 95 years from the time of the first recording. Musicians and record companies claim the copyright protection offered to performers is poor in comparison to that offered in the USA, where recordings are protected for 70 years beyond the death of the performer.

Once the copyright period has passed, items are said to belong in the **public domain**. Anyone can use and adopt those works as they see fit. Alternatively, an author of a document can choose to waive copyright at the time of publication (or any time after) and make their work public domain. Once an item has become public domain it cannot be returned to copyright status.

SAQ 4.3

(a) **In 2006, the BBC broadcast a highly-regarded version of Charles Dickens' 'Bleak House'. Is this television programme copyrighted?**

(b) **Is the Bible copyrighted?**

Answer to SAQ 4.3

(a) Yes it is. Whilst Dickens' original work is no longer under copyright and can be performed by anyone, the BBC adaptation of 'Bleak House' is protected by copyright. In the UK the recording would be protected for 50 years from the date of the first broadcast – that is until 2056.

(b) I admit this is something of a 'trick' question. In almost all parts of the world the Bible is considered to be a public domain publication because it dates from before the concept of copyright. New translations or adaptations of the Bible that make significant changes to the text (such as versions for children) usually are copyrighted by their creators.

However, there is one very specific edition of the Bible that is copyrighted. In the United Kingdom, the King James' Bible (originally printed in 1611) is protected by an indefinite Crown Copyright. Very few other publications have this status, the most famous being the copyright for performances of 'Peter Pan' belonging to the Great Ormond Street Hospital for Sick Children.

EXERCISE 4.3

Do you think long copyright terms are a good idea? Try to think of one reason why copyright should extend for a long time, and one reason why terms should be short. Spend no more than ten minutes on this exercise.

Discussion

One reason for justifying long copyright terms is that most creators only produce a handful of works in their lifetime. Artists in particular cannot be expected to increase their productivity. A long copyright term allows a creator to benefit from their work throughout their lives.

A justification for short terms is that copyright was originally designed to enrich society. Items would enter the public domain where they could be used by anyone in the hope of creating a more literate, better educated and richer society. In fact this idea of copyright was considered so important it was included in the Constitution of the United States. Short terms mean that good ideas are spread more quickly, whilst lengthy copyright terms prevent them being shared with society.

4.2 Digital piracy

When you buy music on CD or a DVD movie – what exactly do you end up owning? The answer is more complicated than you think. You own the case, the printed slip and the physical disc itself, but you do not own the information stored on the disc (the music or movie). The information remains the copyright of the copyright holder – usually either the artist or the studio that published the work. When you buy the disc you are granted a licence to *play* the material. You are not (in the UK at least) permitted to copy, redistribute or edit the information in any way.

Piracy is the illegal duplication of materials that are protected by intellectual property law; it is part of a global counterfeiting industry that costs many billions of pounds every year. Traditionally counterfeiting has been concerned with attempting to copy currencies or luxury goods; but the forgers are increasingly making fakes of other valuable products such as computer memory, life-saving pharmaceuticals and even aircraft components. In many cases these forgeries are of poor quality and have been linked to serious accidents. In 1989 an airliner flying from Oslo to Hamburg crashed into the North Sea killing all 55 people on board. When the wreckage was salvaged it was found that the aircraft had suffered a massive structural failure, caused in part by insufficiently strong counterfeit bolts and fastenings.

One of the most serious piracy problems is the duplication of media – music, movies and computer software. This has been a thriving industry for many years; audio piracy became a problem with the arrival of the cheap cassette recorder in the 1960s, and movie piracy became important with the development of cheap video recorders. Piracy was always limited by three major factors. The first was that it was time consuming to make a copy, few people could duplicate more than one copy at a time and those copies would take a considerable amount of time. The second factor was the quality: copies were invariably inferior to the original. Most people would continue to purchase the original item knowing that they would get a faithful reproduction. Thirdly, gaining access to pirated materials was difficult for people without contacts in the film or music industry, or required them to deal with people on the fringes of criminal culture.

Computer technology has transformed the potential for piracy; at a stroke it has removed the limitations inherent in previous technologies. A computer can make a thousand copies of a piece of digital information in little more time than it takes to make a single copy; and every copy will be an exact duplicate of the original. The internet also provides the perfect distribution method for pirated information. People connect to a website or a file server and download copies directly to their hard disks. There is no need to find a dealer in pirated material; a search engine can do the job.

One of the few remaining restraints on piracy is the sheer size of media files. A CD can hold up to 570MB of information, a DVD can hold over 4GB; and the newer Blu-ray format a staggering 50GB! However, even this restraint can be overcome with digital technology; two novel data formats, MP3 and DivX, allow digital copies – of poorer quality – of a very small size to be made, and so transferred quickly over the internet. Now, almost anyone can receive digital music over their phone line, and with broadband, receiving digital movies is possible.

MP3 – the pirate's friend

MP3 is a format for storing audio data that is extremely useful for legitimate purposes, but it is best known for aiding the pirating of music. MP3 files are small because they are compressed and can be stored on portable devices such as music players, mobile phones and handheld computers where computer memory is limited. The format was invented in Germany, and the algorithm made publicly available. It took little time before people saw the format's potential for transmitting music over the internet.

MP3 software players

You studied MP3 in relation to music in Unit 13. MP3 stands for Moving Picture Expert Group (MPEG) Audio Layer 3. The audio compression system chosen was the third selected by the group – hence Layer 3.

The problem

A CD stores music in a digital format. The original analogue music has been sampled into a stream of digital bits (you have already been introduced to this process in Unit 3). The CD standard requires the original soundtrack to be sampled 44,100 times per second (this is known as the **sample rate**, written as 44.1 kHz). Each sample is 2 bytes (16 bits) long. A separate sample is taken for each of the right and left channels.

EXERCISE 4.4

How many bits are used to store one second of audio on a CD?

─ ─ ─ ─ ─ ─ ─ ─ ─ ─ ─ **Discussion** ─ ─ ─ ─ ─ ─ ─ ─ ─ ─ ─

The text has told us that the sample frequency for a CD is 44,100 samples per second, each sample is comprised of 16 bits and one sample is taken for each of the stereo channels. The answer can be calculated as follows:

44,100 samples per second × 16 bits × 2 channels = 1,411,200 bits.

This and the next three exercises demonstrate how much information can be stored on a music CD.

EXERCISE 4.5

How many bits are there on a full 74-minute CD?

***Hint:* The answer will be the number of bits recorded in one second (which you know from Exercise 4.4) multiplied by the number of seconds in 74 minutes.**

Discussion

There are 74 × 60 = 4,440 seconds in 74 minutes and
1,411,200 bits/second × 4,440 seconds = 6,265,728,000 bits.

EXERCISE 4.6

How many seconds would it take to transmit the number of bits in Exercise 4.5 over a broadband modem running at a maximum speed of 8 million bits per second?

Discussion

The answer is the total number of bits on the disc divided by the number of bits that can be transmitted in one second.

6,265,728,000 bits/8,000,000 bits per second = 783 seconds (about 13 minutes).

Compression programs

Compression as a solution

The size of a file can be reduced by the use of a lossless compression system such as Zip. (Unit 3 discussed compression.) On average such compression can shrink a file to half its original size.

EXERCISE 4.7

Assuming a lossless compression algorithm could be used to compress the music in Exercise 4.5 by 50 per cent, how long would it take to transmit the music over the modem?

Discussion

Half the time, i.e. 392 seconds (about 6½ minutes).

Greater compression can be achieved using lossy algorithms. (You met one, JPEG, in Unit 4.) Lossy algorithms achieve greater compression by discarding some information. MP3 is a lossy algorithm that relies on quirks in human hearing to help achieve its compression. This process is known as **perceptual encoding**. For instance, the human ear is not equally sensitive to all frequencies of sound, therefore the MP3 compression may discard inaudible and less audible frequencies without an appreciable loss of quality. In addition, if a piece of music has two simultaneous sounds, a listener may notice only the louder noise, so MP3 compression may discard the quieter noise.

The quality of MP3 music is subjective. Some people claim to be able to tell the difference between MP3 and the original, others find MP3 as good. MP3 supports different recording qualities; music requiring higher fidelity can be compressed using a higher bit rate at the expense of an increased file size.

Music on a CD can easily be reduced to an MP3 file occupying one-tenth of the original size. Consequently, MP3 files are better suited to transmission over slow networks and allow more files to be transmitted over a given connection.

It is simple to convert conventional CD music into MP3 format using a program known as a **ripper**. The majority of computer programs capable of playing CD audio discs are also able to convert the music into MP3 files.

Ripping programs

Other lossy formats are Windows Media Audio (WMA) format which uses a proprietary audio data compression technology developed by Microsoft, and the audio format RealAudio, developed by RealNetworks.

A related topic to that of audio compression is that of digital video compression. Video files are much larger than those created for audio. As an illustration, you may want to repeat Exercise 4.6 to work out how long it would take to transfer the contents of a Blu-ray disk containing 50 GB of data over the same broadband modem.

Just as in the case of audio, this area has been very much influenced by the development and widespread use of compression formats that allow the transfer of video content over the internet. A suite of such formats has been developed by the Moving Picture Experts Group (MPEG, who also developed MP3), a working group of the International Standards Organisation (ISO). You will have used MPEG perhaps without knowing it – DVD movies are stored in the MPEG-2 format, whilst high-definition television and many internet movies use the more sophisticated MPEG-4 format.

To make matters even more complicated many media formats you might have heard about, such as Windows Media Video or Apple QuickTime, are actually containers for other formats. For instance the sound in an Apple QuickTime movie can be encoded in any of eleven different formats and video in any of more than twenty formats! The QuickTime wrapper is designed to make life simple for consumers; instead of battling with dozens of individual sound and video players, they only need the dedicated QuickTime player which includes software designed to play any of these formats. Microsoft's Windows Media Player and RealNetworks' RealPlayer are designed to do much the same thing.

However, some media formats are proprietary – that is their workings are not available to other companies, which means that we still need more than one media player if we want to access all of the content that is out there.

SAQ 4.4

(a) What is the purpose of applying compression techniques to audio files?

(b) What is the chief difference between lossy and lossless compression?

(c) Name two lossy audio compression algorithms.

Answer to SAQ 4.4

(a) Compression can considerably reduce the time required to transmit an audio file over a network. This can remove one of the remaining protections for copyright materials, their size.

(b) Lossy algorithms discard some of the data (one hopes without much noticeable degradation of quality), whereas lossless algorithms keep all the data intact.

(c) MP3 and Windows Media Audio (or RealAudio).

4.3 The rise and fall of Napster

MP3-encoded music quickly found its way on to the internet. There were hundreds of thousands of people willing to download copies of their favourite music (an activity which may violate copyright), but they found files difficult to find: MP3 files were often given unusual names to disguise their contents from suspicious ISPs and music company investigators.

However everything changed in 1999 with the advent of Napster, the pet project of an American university student, Shawn Fanning. Napster consisted of a small client program downloaded to users' computers and a powerful central database. When someone installed the Napster client on their computer, the software searched their hard disk for MP3 files. As well as the encoded music, an MP3 file includes hidden tags containing information about the recording artist, the album, track names, and so on; by reading these tags, the Napster client was able to correctly identify the music, and send the information back to the central Napster database.

When the user then connected to the internet and ran Napster, the program would inform the central database server that it was available. The Napster database added the client to its list of active users.

Using Napster was straightforward. Users entered the name of a song, album or artist into a search box in the Napster client; the program then sent this information to the central Napster server. The server searched its database of registered Napster users, looking for those who had copies of the music and compared this with the list of Napster users currently online.

If it had a corresponding entry, the server sent the internet addresses of active users who had the requested music direct to the user's client as shown in Figure 4.1.

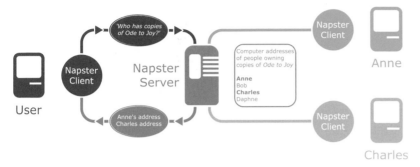

Figure 4.1   Requesting a file from the Napster system. The user's copy of the Napster client sends a request for Beethoven's Ode to Joy to the Napster server. The server checks its database for users possessing Ode to Joy, then looks for those who are currently logged in (Anne and Charles). The internet addresses of these two computers are then sent back to the user's client

The user would see a list of active users and could download a copy of the music simply by clicking one of the entries in the list. The user's Napster client program used the address information provided by the Napster server to make a direct connection to the remote machine's Napster client. Once the connection was established, the music was transferred directly between the two machines without involving the Napster server, as Figure 4.2 illustrates.

Figure 4.2   Downloading a file using Napster. The user chose one of the copies of Ode to Joy belonging to a currently active Napster user (Anne). Their client has made contact with Anne's Napster client

A user could download a number of pieces of music simultaneously. At the same time, their computer could well be sending music to other Napster users. The process was known as **file swapping** or **file sharing**.

Naturally, the music industry considered Napster to be a tool for piracy and took legal action. In their defence, Napster compared their service to a group of friends lending CDs to each other. Indeed, legal advice to Napster was that the company was immune from prosecution (in the USA) under the American Audio Home Recording Act (AHRA) on two grounds:

1   the Act allows purchasers of a CD to make a copy for personal use – such as making a copy for use in the car;

2   the Act allows purchasers to make copies for other people provided that they do not receive any compensation or payment.

Conveniently, the AHRA places no restrictions on the type or number of copies that can be produced from a single recording, nor does it specify to whom those copies may be given. However, it is clear that the AHRA did not intend for thousands of copies to be made from a single recording.

Napster's second defence was that since the music files did not come from the Napster servers themselves, the company could not be prosecuted for piracy. In reality, the weakness in Napster's defence was that they were involved in the process since they maintained the central database of users and MP3 files.

The first action against Napster was brought by members of the music group Metallica. Rather than close the company outright, Metallica sought to have all references to their music removed from the Napster servers. They were followed by other artists, and then by the recording studios themselves. At the time, Napster was hoping to become a successful dot.com business. It needed to attract investors, but these were wary of a company attracting the notice of lawyers.

After a succession of legal setbacks, Napster closed its service and declared itself bankrupt. During Napster's heyday, tens of millions of pieces of music were exchanged every day. Indeed, Napster traffic grew to such an extent that many organisations blocked access to the Napster service for fear that it would prevent normal internet services. After the original service ended, the Napster name was acquired by the Roxio group to rebrand their pressplay online music service. Today Napster is a successful business with several million users paying monthly subscription fees to access millions of pieces of music. Napster's creator, Shawn Fanning, now develops software for online video games.

SAQ 4.5

(a) What were the key aspects of Napster?

(b) What technical problem could cause it to fail?
    Hint: Was there a single, central point of failure?

Answer to SAQ 4.5

(a) Napster's key aspects were:

■   it provided a simple method of finding and downloading music from the internet;

■   users downloaded the Napster client which would handle searches, downloads and uploads;

- client programs searched for the location of music using a large centralised database;

- downloads and uploads involved the direct exchange of files between Napster clients.

(b) The system would fail if the central database was unavailable.

4.4 Peer-to-peer file swapping

Napster was vulnerable to legal action because it held information about its users' music on central servers. More recent file swapping systems have dispensed with the need for these servers and are known as **peer-to-peer** client programs.

Peer-to-peer networks depend on client programs running on each of the network's users' computers. These programs catalogue all of the files on the machine that are available for sharing. The clients then look for fellow programs on the internet. An individual peer-to-peer program will only connect to a few other such programs, but each of them in turn is connected to a few more, which are in turn linked to a few more ...

When a user searches for a file, their client first sends a request to a relatively small number of remote peer-to-peer clients. These programs search their catalogues, then in turn send the request on to the clients they are linked to (referred to as a 'hop'). Within a few hops it is possible to search a very large number of computers for the requested information.

Figure 4.3 shows how this works. The user has instructed their peer-to-peer program to search for Beethoven's *Ode to Joy*. It contacts three other clients running on Alice, Barry and Cathy's computers and looks for the file. In turn, each of those programs contacts three others, running on other computers. Each of these computers performs the same search for *Ode to Joy* and may pass the search on to further computers.

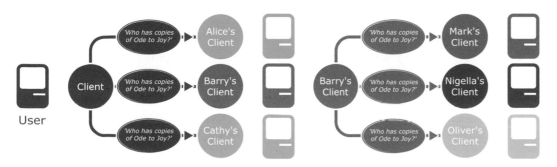

Figure 4.3 A simple peer-to-peer file-sharing program. For simplicity only Barry's peer-to-peer program is shown contacting others running on Mark, Nigella and Oliver's computers

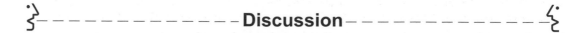

EXERCISE 4.8

If a peer-to-peer program contacts 10 computers with each hop, how many computers can it search in just five hops?

— — — — — — — — — — **Discussion** — — — — — — — — — —

The first hop gives 10 connections, the second 10 for each of these – 10 × 10 = 100, the third 10 times as many – 1000, the fourth another 10 times as many – 10,000, the fifth and last another 10 times as many – 100,000.

This exercise should show you how a fairly modest idea – contacting 10 peers who then each contact 10 – can result in very large numbers very quickly.

Peer-to-peer systems are inefficient in some ways in that they send messages to others without knowing whether the others have the file being requested. The vast majority of messages sent in such a network will not yield the desired result. Although each of these messages is very small, their sheer number – as you saw in the exercise above – results in a huge volume of traffic being generated within a network (which might remind you of the effect of spam email). Fortunately, the number of messages is not allowed to grow indefinitely; the original request can only make a certain number of hops across the network – known as its **time-to-live**. Each time a message is sent to a new client, the request's time-to-live is decremented (decreased by one). When it reaches zero, no further messages will be transmitted.

If the requested piece of information is found on a remote computer, the original user's peer-to-peer client negotiates a direct link to that computer, as shown in Figure 4.4, and downloads the file without having to use any intermediate computers such as the centralised servers used by Napster. A peer-to-peer system such as this allows a user to recover a music file from more than one source. The peer-to-peer client requests different sections of the original file from each remote machine and joins them together on the user's computer. All of this happens without users needing to be aware of how the system works.

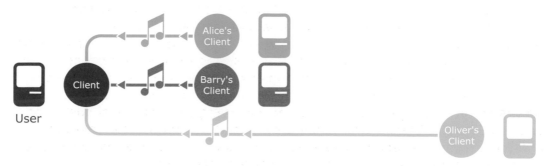

Figure 4.4 Retrieving files using a peer-to-peer system

Peer-to-peer networks are a major problem for media producers as they allow rapid propagation of pirated materials. (Tracks by major artists have been leaked from their recording companies and made available for download even before official release.) Peer-to-peer networks are more difficult to close down than a system such as Napster as there is no identifiable organisation that can be prosecuted or closed down. Worse still, the entire network is ad hoc: as people log in and off, the 'network' itself changes. Material that is available at one moment may not be there five minutes later, a file may have moved to another computer, or could have been copied a thousand times.

While peer-to-peer systems may only seem to be useful for piracy they do have some fundamental advantages over client–server systems. Typically, information in client–server systems is held on one or a small group of servers. When these servers receive a very large number of requests this can reduce the service's response speed or even cause it to crash. Peer-to-peer systems make hundreds of copies of information spread across the entire internet, spreading and thereby reducing the risk to parts of the system. They have been used to distribute software patches for operating systems, anti-virus programs and are now even being used to distribute legal copies of movies, television programmes and music.

Peer-to-peer networks are extremely resistant to deliberate damage such as denial of service attacks (see Unit 14). Information that is widely distributed can still be propagated even if most copies of that information are unobtainable. With governments and industry deeply concerned about the prospect of 'cyber-terrorism' being used to target vital resources, it may be essential to rebuild the internet using a peer-to-peer approach.

BBC iPlayer

In late 2007, the BBC released its iPlayer service which allows internet users to play BBC television and radio programmes over the internet at a time of their choosing. The service has two components: a streaming service where a user chooses a programme and watches it there and then, and a download service (as of early 2008 this was only available to users of Microsoft Windows), where users could copy programmes to their hard disks for later viewing within a restricted time period of the download.

The download service employs peer-to-peer technology to reduce the load on the central BBC iPlayer servers and to improve the speed of downloads to individual users. However, many ISPs have become concerned that the popularity of iPlayer is affecting their financial future. As you learned earlier, ISPs buy network capacity based on the expected usage of their customers; iPlayer has created an enormous spike in demand for network capacity – in its first month alone, iPlayer was responsible for *doubling* the price ISPs had to pay for network access. ISPs are faced with an unenviable choice; increasing their charge to customers or absorbing the additional costs and reducing their profitability. Whichever decision they choose to make, the problem is going to become more acute as more online video services are launched to more customers and in increased resolution.

BitTorrent

A well-known example of a peer-to-peer network is BitTorrent. It consists of distributed clients running on individual networked computers. Perhaps confusingly, BitTorrent is the name of the company founded by its creator, Bram Cohen, as well as the name for the protocol that is used by a large number of other programs. In this discussion we will be concerned with the workings of the general BitTorrent system.

It's been a while, so let us return to the two internet users Alice and Bob. If Alice wishes to distribute a file through BitTorrent, she is said to create a **seed**. Alice will use software (often distributed with a BitTorrent client) to break her file into smaller chunks (ranging from 64kb to 4Mb in size).

SAQ 4.6

Alice has a 100 Mb file which is to be distributed via BitTorrent in 64 kb chunks. How many chunks will be created?

Answer to SAQ 4.6

100Mb = (1024 × 100) kb = 102,400 kb

102,400 kb / 64 kb = 1,600 chunks.

Each of the chunks is then identified by applying a cryptographic hash (see Unit 14, Section 3.2) which is stored in a new **torrent file**.

SAQ 4.7

What is the purpose of the hash?

Answer to SAQ 4.7

A hash uniquely identifies a piece of data. Each of the chunks will have a unique identifier allowing it to be recognised on the BitTorrent network.

As well as the hashes, the **torrent** file might contain information about the creator of the torrent; and if it is a movie or album, names of artists, publishers, etc. Alice's relatively small torrent file can now be uploaded to a torrent server or to a website.

When Bob wishes to download Alice's file, he first obtains a copy of the torrent and loads it into his own BitTorrent client. Bob's client now has a complete list of all the unique identifiers for the chunks, it only needs to find the chunks themselves. Bob's client then negotiates with another BitTorrent client on a remote machine called the **tracker**, which holds records of the identities of all the clients currently sharing the requested file.

The tracker provides Bob's BitTorrent client with the addresses of a number of other clients that hold some, or all, of the chunks belonging to Alice's file. Bob's client then makes direct links to each of these clients and begins downloading random chunks of the whole file. When it has finished downloading a chunk, Bob's client makes a request for the addresses of further chunks and so on until it has received all the chunks; at which point it assembles the chunks back into a perfect copy of the original document.

EXERCISE 4.9

Can you think of a reason why BitTorrent clients download a random selection of the available chunks?

── Discussion ──

It is done to speed up the distribution of files and reduce the demand on Alice's computer. Suppose Alice has a file split into six chunks (we will number them *1*, *2*, *3*, *4*, *5* and *6*). Bob's client randomly chooses chunks *1*, *2* and *4* and begins to download them. Charles then logs on to the BitTorrent network and begins to download Alice's file; his client randomly chooses chunks *3*, *4* and *6*. When Bob and Charles' clients have downloaded their first set of chunks they will request further chunks from the tracker. Instead of referring it back to Alice's computer, the tracker can direct Bob's client to Charles' machine for the missing chunks *3* and *6*, whilst Charles' client can receive *1* and *2* from Bob. They both now have five of the six available chunks. In the meantime, Alice's client could have sent chunk *5* to yet another client.

In a BitTorrent system, Bob is not merely a downloader, his client is also uploading chunks to other users. Each time Bob downloads a chunk, his client informs the tracker of the identity of the chunk and Bob's address and will provide it to other users in the system.

As more and more users join a BitTorrent network, the mean speed of sharing files increases, making it a very efficient way of sharing files and highly resilient to denial-of-service attacks. BitTorrent encourages people to upload chunks from their computers by penalising those who only download (so-called **leechers**) with slower download speeds.

BitTorrent has proved to be a very controversial technology and has had a profound effect on how the internet is used. A survey, conducted in late 2007, estimated that the BitTorrent protocol consumed the largest share of internet capacity, ranging from 49 per cent of all traffic in the Middle East, to 84 per cent in Eastern Europe; rising to an astounding 95 per cent of all traffic at night! (ipoque Internet Survey 2007, ipoque GmbH, 2007). BitTorrent has become by far the most important technique for sharing pirated materials, so much so that many ISPs have started to identify BitTorrent users and to restrict their service, or terminate their connections. However, BitTorrent has many legitimate uses, including:

- software upgrades and bug fixes for the online video game World of Warcraft;

- Amazon's S3 internet storage service to make files available to large numbers of users;

- obtaining legitimate movies and music through Bram Cohen's BitTorrent Inc.

SAQ 4.8

(a) **Why was Napster *not* an example of a true peer-to-peer system?**

(b) **What advantages does a peer-to-peer system have over a typical client–server system?**

Answer to SAQ 4.8

(a) Napster relied on its powerful central database to store information about the music files held on individual user's machines. All users had to connect to the database before they could use Napster.

(b) Peer-to-peer systems are less vulnerable to failure or deliberate attack because the distribution of information is such that there is no single vulnerable point. The interconnections change constantly.

4.5   Evading control?

Many political and campaigning movements have flourished on the web, spreading their message to a large audience. Some of their opponents have attempted to prevent the dissemination of a message by many means, including persecution of the sender.

This raises the question, is it possible to hide the traffic from file-sharing systems, or to provide anonymity for the participants or confidentiality for the content?

In an attempt to at least hide the file-sharing traffic, encryption of the protocol traffic is available on some implementations of the BitTorrent protocol. The main motivation for this is that some ISPs try to throttle BitTorrent traffic because of its high overall bandwidth usage, and the encryption manages to hide the traffic to some degree. Note however that the encryption of the protocol messages does not provide confidentiality of the file content that is shared, since anyone with an interest in this file content can just use the protocol to download it (be it law enforcement officers investigating a copyright infringement or intelligence officers from an undemocratic state investigating political opposition). Also, it does not provide anonymity of the people who download files, since the messages can still be traced from their source to their destination.

To deal with this insecurity (in situations where one would view it as an insecurity), one possibility is to use file-sharing in combination with general mechanisms that enable anonymous internet communications. As you learned in the previous unit, it is quite possible for a malicious individual to intercept data as it crosses the internet, and from that, to determine which sites a user chooses to visit and with whom they communicate.

There are a number of technologies available to enable anonymous internet communications, the best known of which is called Tor. Like BitTorrent, Tor is itself built on the concept of peer-to-peer networks. It is the aim of these anonymity networks such as Tor to make it difficult or impossible to monitor individual users.

In the case of Tor, this is achieved as follows. Every time a user sends a request to view a web page, rather than sending the request directly to the relevant server, the user submits the request in an encrypted form to the peer-to-peer Tor network. Tor chooses one client in the network at random. This new peer then submits the request for the page to the remote server. The page's content is then directed back to the original requester. To prevent the server locating the computer that made the original request, the data is first encrypted then routed back through the peer-to-peer Tor network along a complex path.

EXERCISE 4.10

Can you think of a disadvantage of using an anonymiser such as Tor?

Discussion

The biggest disadvantage is the serious overhead imposed by Tor. It forces computers to work harder by encrypting and decrypting data as it enters and leaves the network, and introduces unavoidable delays by routing information via other Tor users.

Since anonymous communication can be used for purposes that might be considered legitimate, and also those that are illegitimate, anonymity networks have provoked a certain degree of controversy. The development of several such networks has received financial support from public sources (including the US Naval Research Lab). Legitimate purposes to which they can be put include to support (and protect) the work of dissidents in undemocratic countries. On the other hand, accusations have been made by law enforcement agencies that these types of network are used for illegal purposes such as the download of child pornography. It was reported that

Tor servers were the target of a series of police investigations in Germany in 2006. Another anonymity network, Java Anon Proxy (JAP), was also investigated in Germany in 2003. As you learned in our discussion of cryptography, in this unit and Unit 14, security technology is always a two-edged sword; it offers great benefits to society, but it can also produce new threats to that society.

EXERCISE 4.11

A hypothetical government proposes to outlaw security technologies such as encryption and anonymous networks. Give one benefit of such a policy and one drawback. Do not spend more than ten minutes on this exercise.

Discussion

An advantage of outlawing encryption is that all internet traffic could be examined for illegal content which would make law enforcement very much easier than at present.

A disadvantage is that everyone's personal information would be exposed to attack as it travelled over the network. Since the internet cannot be considered secure, this is a very serious threat.

4.6 Summary

Digital technologies make it easy to produce materials such as music or graphics for sale and to sell them via the web. This means that copyright infringement in the form of piracy is equally easy.

Piracy is the large-scale reproduction of entire works without payment to the originator. Formats such as MP3 enable piracy using the internet. We looked at Napster, which provided a form of 'brokering' service to people willing to exchange music. While the owners of Napster assumed they had circumvented the law, their central database was deemed to make them accessories to piracy.

We examined peer-to-peer networking and saw that it has one general advantage: robustness. We chose BitTorrent as an example of peer-to-peer networking and explored its operation in some detail. BitTorrent is an excellent example of a software application which has positive benefits, but which also aids the illegal distribution of copyright materials.

Finally, we saw how peer-to-peer networks can enable anonymous internet communications such as the Tor network. In each of these cases, we saw that there were legitimate and illegal uses of these technologies.

5 Attempting total control

Section 4 described how free access to personal information affects the individual. In this section you will study how free access to information is being seen as an affront to the commercial concerns of organisations, and the response of these organisations in attempting to control *how* their products are used.

This is a fundamental change in the way consumers use goods and services. Traditionally a producer's relationship with a consumer ends when the user purchases the product; for instance, when you buy a book you may simply read the book, you can mark pages with notes, tear out pages, give the book to a friend or even burn the book.

When we buy a CD we consider it to be ours to do with as we wish. Whether we play the music, turn the contents into MP3 files or even use the disc as a coaster, the producer has no direct control over how we use or misuse the product (but remember we could violate copyright law by making copies of the music on the disc).

However, it is now possible to use software to control access to a product – the manufacturer can stipulate just how their product is to be used; the type of equipment it is compatible with, whether it can be copied, altered or even who can use the product.

This section is concerned with the concept of digital rights management (DRM). It aims to:

■   introduce the concept of DRM;

■   show how DRM can protect copyrighted data;

■   demonstrate the weaknesses of DRM systems;

■   illustrate a proposal to use DRM to improve computer security;

■   discuss the ethical aspects of the use of DRM.

5.1 Digital rights management

Digital rights management (DRM) is a concept whereby the original publisher of material retains control of how that material is accessed. This control may be systems to prevent a user copying material on to a disc or their computer, blocking conversion to MP3, or systems that require the user to pay each time they access the material.

Highly sophisticated forms of DRM are now under discussion. The rise of MP3 and Napster encouraged record and video companies to investigate techniques capable of preventing piracy. The most mature technique was the Secure Digital Music Initiative (SDMI), developed by a consortium of hardware and software manufacturers.

Secure Digital Music Initiative (SDMI)   (Optional)

To date almost all attempts at controlling the use of copyright material have failed because any security was restricted to only part of the system. The **Secure Digital Music Initiative (SDMI)** was an attempt to secure all parts of the music market, including the hardware for playing and recording music and the recordings themselves. SDMI was an industry body comprising all the major electronics manufacturers, the record publishers and software companies.

Aims of SDMI

SDMI aimed to discourage piracy by preventing hardware or software music players from duplicating materials. One important requirement was that any system would have to be capable of working with old players and recordings; it was unacceptable to introduce a new format that would render most people's music libraries obsolete.

It would have been easier to develop a completely new hardware format and issue music on that, but companies already had considerable investment in the CD manufacturing processes and recognised that it would take a long time for new music formats to become established in the marketplace.

The insistence that SDMI be compatible with existing systems ensured that the proposal was always going to be a compromise; in fact, it was the weakness that undermined the whole endeavour. Lacking a new hardware solution, SDMI's security needed to rely on software: the music would be protected by a series of **digital watermarks**.

Digital watermarks

A watermark is often used to establish the authenticity of paper documents. The mark is impressed into the paper during the manufacturing process and cannot be altered or removed without damaging the document. Bank notes often use a watermark that is only revealed when they are held up to the light.

Digital watermarks are streams of bits added to the informational bits in a file when it is created. Ideally the watermark is undetectable during normal use, but it can be retrieved using specialised software. SDMI used two watermarks in every file. The first was known as the **robust watermark**. The robust watermark would survive compression, decompression, changes in file format and copying between devices – even if the machines were not themselves SDMI compliant.

The robust watermark indicated that a file was SDMI compatible and therefore not intended for copying. When an SDMI file was played in a suitable player, the player would look for the robust watermark. If it found one it would look for a second watermark – the **fragile watermark**.

The fragile watermark would not survive the process of being copied, compressed or altered; i.e. any copies made from an SDMI master would lack the fragile watermark but retain the robust watermark, indicating that the music was protected under SDMI. A player presented with an SDMI file without a fragile watermark might refuse to play the music.

The watermarks were placed in the audible component of the data to ensure that the robust watermark would be copied, even if the copy was made using a non-SDMI machine. The fragile watermark would be lost in the copying process preventing the pirate copies being played on SDMI machines.

EXERCISE 5.1   (OPTIONAL)

How would this approach affect the use of pirated material on non-SDMI compliant hardware?

─────────────── Discussion ───────────────

It would have no effect, since older machines would lack the SDMI watermark checking process. Pirated SDMI materials could still have been played on older players. The music industry would have relied on the continual replacement of older machines by newer SDMI-compliant hardware, gradually eliminating the pirate market.

As the watermarks were placed in the audible component of the data, they made changes to it, which implies that SDMI music was not a true recording of the original. SDMI proponents were confident that these changes were so small that they were undetectable and were far smaller than the distortions induced by faults in the physical structure of the disc or noise in the listener's hi-fi system.

Creating an SDMI world

The SDMI Consortium constructed a strategy for introducing the technology in two phases. The first phase (phase 1) was to introduce SDMI players and music into the commercial market. During this time, the vast majority of players and recorders would not be SDMI-compliant and the user would not have noticed any change to the way they use music.

With time, as SDMI became more common, the industry would introduce phase 2 of SDMI. Phase 2 was intended to tempt users into buying SDMI-compliant equipment by issuing titles with special features such as bonus tracks, interviews, and discounts against further purchases. There were also plans to issue music over the internet on a pay-per-listen basis.

Phase 2 would have been introduced by including special data on music discs. When one of these titles was placed into an SDMI-compliant player, the player would read the data and inform the user that phase 2 SDMI was available. If the user chose to upgrade, they would download the phase 2 software either from the disc or over the internet. If they chose not to upgrade to phase 2 SDMI, they could continue to use their existing collection of music as before, but would be unable to access any of the phase 2 extras. Naturally, any players or recorders issued after the beginning of phase 2 would have had the features enabled by default.

SDMI – was the system fatally flawed?

SDMI would stand or fall on the strength of its watermark system. And it contained a weakness: the compatibility requirement.

If an SDMI player found no watermark, it would be programmed to assume that the music was recorded before the advent of SDMI and was not protected. (The alternative strategy, that an SDMI player would not play a piece of music without a watermark, would have made people's music collections obsolete overnight.) Therefore, any file without recognisable SDMI watermarks would not be considered to be an SDMI file.

If the watermark could be removed from an SDMI file, or the watermark was altered sufficiently to lose its identity then the document would no longer be considered to be an SDMI file and therefore no longer under SDMI control. Without SDMI control, the file could be copied and distributed.

The SDMI Consortium was so confident of their watermarking system that in September 2000 they issued a challenge to the computing community known as HackSDMI.

The HackSDMI challenge

The HackSDMI Challenge was actually split into six sub-challenges (A to F), four of which were concerned with watermarking. Since the HackSDMI Challenge was extremely technical we shall only discuss the first sub-challenge known as *Sub-challenge A*.

Entrants to the HackSDMI Challenge were given three pieces of music:

song 1 – a piece of music without any SDMI watermarks;

song 2 – the same as song 1, but with the SDMI watermarks;

song 3 – a different piece of music also containing the SDMI watermarks.

To win the challenge, it was necessary either to entirely remove the watermarks from song 3 or to render them useless so that the song would lose its SDMI protection.

The 'simplest' attack on SDMI attempted to isolate the watermarks. Songs 1 and 2 only differed in that song 2 contained the watermark. The researchers sampled the songs and for each interval compared the information in song 2 with that in song 1. Any difference had to be due to the SDMI watermark. 'Subtracting' the difference from song 2 removed the watermark.

The researchers were then able to remove the watermark from song 3. Since they already had the SDMI watermark, they were able to 'subtract' that information from song 3 to produce an unprotected version of the music.

The results of HackSDMI

In October 2000 the online magazine *Salon* reported that SDMI had been comprehensively defeated. At first the story was denied by the SDMI Consortium, but by the end of October it was clear that SDMI was in serious trouble. A team from Princeton University publicly claimed to have broken SDMI using a variety of techniques. They had made an attempt on all six sub-challenges and were satisfied that they had had succeeded in all of them.

The HackSDMI Challenge had a sting in its tail. Participants in the challenge had to sign non-disclosure agreements with the SDMI Consortium preventing them from publishing their work. This had incensed many researchers who publicly called for non-cooperation.

The Princeton team announced that they would present their work at a computer security conference. The team's lawyers warned that they might be vulnerable to prosecution. The US Digital Millennium Copyright Act (DMCA) forbids people from circumventing copy-protection systems. While the HackSDMI Challenge could be seen as research, publication of the work would allow anyone to copy the Princeton techniques and defeat SDMI. The warning was reinforced by a letter from the SDMI Consortium threatening prosecution should the team publish. The Princeton team withdrew the paper from the conference.

The team were so worried about prosecution that they turned to a judge, asking for protection from prosecution should they publish their work. This was almost unheard of in the United States. The case attracted enormous public attention and the support of the Electronic Frontier Foundation.

The Electronic Frontier Foundation

The Electronic Frontier Foundation (EFF) is an organisation committed to educating the public and legislators on technological issues. The EFF is concerned with the effects of new technology on people's rights and has campaigned on issues such as cryptography, telephone-tapping, censorship and copyright.

EFF

The EFF argues many cases on the grounds that the American Constitution provides certain freedoms to the population. Although the EFF is largely concerned with developments in the USA, its campaigning stance has been copied by other organisations around the world.

The SDMI team relented; by August 2001, the Recording Industry Association of America said it had no objection to the work being published. The Princeton team presented their work to a second computing conference and their paper was published on the web.

The description above is greatly simplified. If you are interested in HackSDMI you may wish to refer to the academic paper written by the Princeton team. **You are not expected to read this paper for the course!**

The HackSDMI
Challenge paper

The end of SDMI

As if the results of the HackSDMI Challenge were not devastating enough, internal bickering ensured that the SDMI Consortium quickly fell apart. Officially SDMI has been put on hold since May 2001, although few people expect it to ever see the light of day.

Other examples of broken DRM systems   (Optional)

More generally, so far the history of DRM systems has been to a significant extent a history of broken security mechanisms.

Another example is that of the Content Scrambling System (CSS). It is a DRM system introduced in 1996 which is used on many commercially produced DVD-Video discs. The content of the disc is encrypted with a symmetric key encryption algorithm which turned out to be relatively weak. It was compromised in 1999 when the Norwegian reverse engineering expert Jon Lech Johansen released the computer program DeCSS which is capable of decrypting the CSS content. Johansen was subsequently taken to court by the Norwegian economic crime unit Oekokrim, following a complaint by the US DVD Copy Control Association and the Motion Picture Association. Johansen denied writing the decryption code in DeCSS and argued that he had not obtained any illegal information since he owned the relevant DVDs himself, and that according to Norwegian law it is legal to make copies for personal use. Johansen was acquitted of all charges in 2003.

Another program for breaking the CSS encryption was released in 1999 by the international underground software cracking group DrinkOrDie. Legal proceedings were launched against this group in 2001 based on information from a member of the group who worked undercover for US Customs. The Australian alleged co-leader of the group was charged with copyright infringement and conspiracy to commit copyright infringement under US legislation. After a three-year legal battle in Australia, he was extradited to the USA in early February 2007 where he was sentenced to 51 months in prison. The American alleged co-leader was sentenced to 46 months, which was later reduced to 18 months for his cooperation, which led to further sentencing of 21 other US-based group members with sentences up to 41 months in jail each in 2002 and 2003. Six further group members were arrested in Britain, of whom three were sentenced and a fourth deported to Russia.

A more recent example for a broken DRM system is that of Apple's FairPlay technology, which is built into the QuickTime multimedia software and is used by several of Apple's multimedia products and services such as the iPhone, iPod, iTunes, and iTunes Store. It is used to encrypt audio files using the AES algorithm (see Unit 14) in combination with the cryptographic hash function MD5. There were several attempts on circumventing this DRM system that were at least temporarily successful. The most well-known one is the open source application QTFairUse written by Jon Johansen (who also distributed the DeCSS program). It allows one to remove the encryption of the FairPlay system and was created by reverse engineering the encryption algorithm. Possibly as a reaction to the continuing successes in breaking DRM systems, Apple started to sell audio files not protected by DRM in 2007.

Another recent example is the case of the Advanced Access Content System (AACS), whose specification was released in 2005 with the goal to restrict access to the content of high-definition HD-DVD and Blu-ray discs. Again, AACS encrypts the digital content using the AES encryption algorithm. The difference from earlier systems such as CSS is that now each media player has its own unique decryption key, which allows companies to disable the decryption key of a specific player if it becomes compromised. The first devices making use of AACS became available in 2006 and within months the first decryption keys had been extracted by crackers from weakly protected players. In April 2007 the compromised keys were revoked by the AACS consortium.

Sometimes, DRM mechanisms do not only turn out to be weak in themselves, but they threaten the security of the PCs that are used to play the digital content, without warning to the legitimate customers. An example is a copy protection system called Extended Copy Protection (XCP) used by Sony BMG on about 100 of their music CDs in 2005. The software automatically installed itself on any Windows PC that played the CDs. In November 2005, the US Computer Emergency Response Team (CERT, part of the US Department of Homeland Security) released a warning that this software may be a security threat to the user PCs. Sony then recalled the CDs from merchants and offered to exchange affected CDs for unprotected CDs. At the same time, the state of Texas brought legal action against Sony BMG because of the copy protection system, which was the first suit filed with regards to the Texas spyware law from 2005. Also, class action suits were filed against Sony BMG which reached settlements by January 2007, including one which required Sony BMG to pay up to $150 for any damages caused to each customer's PC when trying to remove the spyware.

Hackers and crackers

We discussed the difference between the two terms in the previous unit. A cracker is an individual who attacks a computer for criminal purposes, a hacker does so for legal reasons.

DRM systems can be broken by sufficiently knowledgeable attackers. In some cases crackers have examined the interaction of the DRM with the computer's operating system and hardware and have been able to remove the links between the media files and the DRM systems. In others, they have hunted through computer memory as the DRM system runs and found the necessary encryption keys which they have then distributed over the internet. Many DRM systems have been defeated because they have one fatal flaw – at some point, the encrypted file has to be decrypted so that it can be sent to video displays or to loudspeakers. It is relatively easy to intercept this unencrypted data and produce an unprotected version of the media file that can be recorded and distributed. Media and hardware companies are trying to prevent this attack by adding a further layer of DRM – this time to encrypt data as it streams between devices. Most recent DVD players, amplifiers, monitors and televisions, and all Blu-ray and HD-DVD players, are equipped with 'High Definition Multimedia Interface' (HDMI) sockets which are protected using a form of encryption known as High-bandwidth Digital Content Protection (HDCP). Ironically, HDCP was responsible for many problems to early adopters of HDMI and the technology has already proven vulnerable to attack.

With current technology, it is generally not possible for a DRM system to notice that its execution is being compromised. That is, the software is vulnerable because it can be tricked into running in a hostile environment. This has motivated the development of a technological foundation for operating systems that allow the software producer to restrict the execution of the software to hardware environments considered trustworthy by the software producer. This technology is the topic of our next section.

HD-DVD was a rival high-definition disc format to Blu-ray. Developed by a consortium including Toshiba and Microsoft, it failed to attract backing from most movie studios – in part because it offered weaker DRM than Blu-ray. The format was abandoned in February 2008.

5.2 Digital rights management hasn't gone away

Public advocacy groups such as the Electronic Frontier Foundation have broadened the debate on DRM by raising the possibility that DRM techniques could be used to infringe privacy, 'profile' individuals or institute differential pricing. Its widespread adoption may also prevent the development of **open source software** and the release of works into the public domain.

DRM would have a serious impact on **fair use**: an exemption in law that allows people to use copyrighted material 'for ... criticism, comment, news reporting, teaching (including multiple copies for classroom use), scholarship, or research' (US Copyright Act 1976, Section 107). An example of fair use is that you are permitted to include small pieces of copyright work in your answers to questions set in this course. Information about how to credit the use of copyright materials is included with each TMA and can also be found on the Assignments section of the M150 website under the heading 'Citing References Helpsheet'.

Open source software is software made available for free distribution. Distribution must not discriminate against persons, groups or fields of endeavour. The software must include source code, and freely allow modification or derivation.

National libraries have been especially critical of DRM. In the UK, all publishers are obliged to deposit at least one copy of every new title with the British Library so that it can be accessed free-of-charge by anyone who asks. This has traditionally not been a problem; books are stored at the library and can be lent out or relevant pieces reproduced. DRM can prevent this – it can restrict the ability of a library to lend a title to another library or individual and it can also prevent sections being reproduced – even for legitimate reasons.

A more subtle problem for libraries is that the DRM technology itself may become obsolete; either being superseded by new DRM, or abandoned entirely. In such circumstances, titles might become effectively locked behind strong encryption and useless to anybody.

Despite the widespread failure of DRM systems as reported in the previous section, the appeal of these technologies is such that a range of companies are developing their own DRM technologies.

Microsoft is the most ambitious of these companies. It has added DRM to its Windows Media Player, and has proposals to include such features in future versions of Microsoft Windows. The proposals, known as **Next-Generation Secure Computing Base (NGSCB)**, were introduced in 2002 under the more innocent name of Palladium. NGSCB would allow software vendors to control the way information is processed inside a computer. The ostensible reason for NGSCB is to increase computer security by preventing malicious software from infecting computers.

Once the operating system had started, the NGSCB enforcement system would take control of the computer. NGSCB contains a feature that will only allow a program to run if it has a corresponding valid digital signature. (You studied digital signatures in Unit 14.) If a program does not have a digital signature, NGSCB could refuse to execute the program entirely. By default, Microsoft intended to ship NGSCB with this feature disabled, but the user would be able to switch it on at any time. Indeed, it is quite likely that many users would only trust programs that have been signed.

In theory, NGSCB could make computing much safer. The viruses and worms of today would not be able to obtain a digital signature certificate; therefore they could never run on a computer that required certification. Of course, many thousands of older applications will also lack a certificate and would also not run on a NGSCB system that required them. If nothing else, NGSCB could encourage an enormous number of software and hardware upgrades!

However, NGSCB may prove to be very restrictive; as an example, the publishers of a particular DVD movie or piece of music could ensure that it could only be played with a particular piece of software or only played a certain number of times. Furthermore, at present, there is no way of policing the necessary certificates. The certificate is a badge of trust; if the NGSCB system encounters a valid signature it automatically trusts the application. However, Microsoft has made it quite clear that signing authorities would not be responsible for the safety of any certified code; these authorities will only be certifying that *they* were satisfied the code met certain minimum standards. The responsibility for the safety of the code would remain with the original author. In theory any company could certify NGSCB applications; it would be up to the user to decide whether they trust the organisation issuing the digital certificate. So it is not impossible to imagine a corrupt organisation issuing NGSCB certificates to virus writers or developers of spyware.

As of 2008, the most recent version of Microsoft Windows (the Vista family) does not include all of the features of NGSCB described above. Many of the features were abandoned as their development would have delayed the introduction of Windows Vista; however, some of NGSCB's functionality is available in certain versions of Windows Vista. For example, the Ultimate and Enterprise editions of Windows Vista include the application BitLocker, which uses a dedicated cryptographic chip (the Trusted Platform Module) and the AES encryption technology (discussed in Unit 14) to store an encrypted version of every single file on a disk, decrypting data only when requested by the user or the operating system.

BitLocker is intended to protect data not just during every day use, but also in the event a computer is stolen, and also when a computer is disposed of. Starting from 2006, many new laptop models and some desktop computers now include a TPM chip, even if its functionality is not supported by the operating system installed on that machine.

SAQ 5.1

Summarise the main points of the DRM debate. (You should strive for at least two points.)

Answer to SAQ 5.1

My points are as follows.

- A tension exists between the 'rights' of a purchaser to use (or abuse) their purchase as they see fit and the 'rights' of a copyright holder to protect their material from certain types of misuse (such as copying for purposes of piracy or 'giving away' the product freely to others).

- The techniques involved in DRM could easily be abused by commercial interests to aid profiling and differential pricing; the guarantees against this are (at present) weak or non-existent.

- As a side-effect, DRM techniques may inhibit or prohibit fair use and the development, exchange and use of open source software.

You may have thought of others, or expressed these differently.

5.3   The problem with digital rights management

DRM allows a copyright holder to control access to their product; if this control is poorly implemented, it conflicts with a person's right to use that product. Ideally DRM should impact as little on the legitimate user as possible – under no circumstances should a person paying for a product receive an inferior product to a person using a pirate version.

Sony has interests in audio-visual equipment, computing and music publishing. Sony's electronic division would clearly benefit from additional sales of computers and players capable of using MP3 files, but its recording arm would be hurt by the illicit exchange of MP3 music.

Sony developed a pair of related DRM technologies: OpenMG™ and MagicGate™. Among other tasks, OpenMG™ converts music from MP3 format into Sony's proprietary ATRAC format – preventing it from being used on non-Sony devices and reducing the potential for piracy.

Sony also chose to protect their material by using proprietary hardware; their music players used a form of storage developed by Sony known as White MemoryStick™. White MemoryStick™ includes a dedicated microchip running the MagicGate™ DRM software. MagicGate™ software permits people to make copies of music on to a portable device, but restricts their abilities to transfer that music onto other computers. MagicGate™ can also be used to control how many times a piece of music is copied or even played.

Figure 5.1 Sony's White MemoryStick™ which is a form of computer memory that can be plugged into a wide variety of devices including computers, camcorders and digital cameras. The White MemoryStick™ format was developed especially for Sony music players

Sony's solution has proved unpopular with users who have been put off by the time-consuming conversion of MP3 files into ATRAC format before they can play their music.

Sony is starting to address the problem and appears to be aware that users want convenience above all else. More recently, they have abandoned some of the most intrusive digital rights management by designing music players that can read more common formats such as MP3 and that use more common memory formats.

> Our intent is to provide rich content and services to users without any frustration, without any stress. Initially, because of our content group, we tried to protect the rights of labels and artists too much, so this made it very difficult for consumers to use the machine. Now we know that for the industry to grow, we have to find an optimum balance point. We have to consider ease of use for consumers but at the same time protect content holders' rights. We think it's almost an advantage for Sony that we have both – we can understand the content side and we have hardware, so we can start thinking about this way ahead.
>
> (Kunitake Ando, President and Chief Operating Officer of the Sony Corporation, November 2002)

A far simpler example of DRM is used by the Apple iPod™ MP3 player preventing it from being used to exchange music.

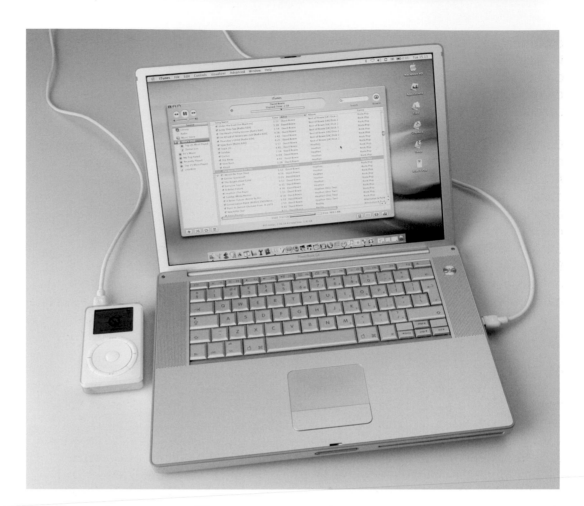

Figure 5.2   The Apple iPod™ MP3 player connected to a computer

While the iPod™ can *play* music, it requires a computer to produce the MP3 files. When a user downloads music from their computer onto an iPod™, the music files are 'tagged' with an identifier unique to that computer. If a user then plugs the iPod™ into a second computer and attempts to transfer music from the iPod™ to the second computer they will not succeed. The identity tag of the second computer will not correspond to the tag of the first computer. The iPod™ will refuse to upload music in this circumstance.

Since users usually want to store music on the iPod™ rather than on their hard disks this does not affect the manner in which people use their music collections. Despite this, programs have been released that defeat the iPod's copy protection software, allowing users to upload music to any computer.

There are further disadvantages arising from DRM systems even for the legitimate users. Some of these were identified by the *Gowers Review of Intellectual Property* which was commissioned by the UK Treasury (Gowers, 2006). For example, DRM systems may prevent activities that should be permitted according to exceptions provided by the law. For instance, Adobe eBooks often have their accessibility settings disabled, which prevents visually impaired readers from making copies in a format which is accessible to them, as permitted by the UK Copyright Act 2002. As noted by the British Library, this kind of problem holds for the great majority of agreements relating to electronic licences. In many countries, including the USA and several European countries (with plans to introduce this in the UK), noncommercial copying by consumers of their own media for private purposes is legal. (However, one is usually not allowed to circumvent DRM systems to do so.) To compensate for this, many countries (but not the UK) raise a copyright levy (tax) at the sale of recording equipment and blank recording media.

Content providers have used DRM systems to discriminate between users in different locations. An example reported by Gowers (2006) was that the Apple iTunes store charged UK-based users 79p for a single music track, but customers in the Eurozone only the equivalent of 68p. To enforce this price discrimination, the iTunes stores operating in a given country only accepted credit cards issued by banks in that country. This was viewed as a breach of European law which aims to prevent barriers of trade between different European countries. To forestall an enquiry and the possibility of multi-million pound fines, in January 2008, Apple announced that it would try to harmonise prices across the EU. Similarly, Video DVDs and Blu-ray discs are usually protected by a so-called region code which only allows the disc to be used within the region for which the DVD player or computer is configured.

As a reaction to what is perceived as unfair practices based on DRM systems, there have been several cases of legal actions by customer rights organisations against industry. For example, the Consumer Council Norway raised a complaint in 2006 against the iTunes Music Store in which it criticises the fact that music downloaded from the iTunes Music Store can only be played on an iPod. Although this DRM based restriction can be circumvented by copying the file to a CD and then ripping it back onto the PC, circumventing the DRM mechanisms is not permitted by the iTunes Terms of Services. According to the terms, the user is only authorised to use the music on up to five iTunes-authorised devices at any time. Also, according to the terms, iTunes reserves the right to make use of the DRM system to unilaterally change the user permissions on content already purchased. For example, in 2006 it was only possible to copy the files onto a maximum of 7 CDs, and this also applied retrospectively to files bought before this rule was introduced. The terms also deny any liability for damage that might arise if a security vulnerability is introduced on a customer's PC by using the iTunes software (as happened in the case of the Sony BMG DRM system XCP discussed earlier).

Other examples of annoyances to customers from DRM systems include the problem that it may be impossible to play certain audio CDs on certain kinds of CD players. Consumers are advised to pay attention to whether there are related warnings printed on the CD and should complain to a customer rights organisation in case of problems that occur without warning.

Because of all these problems, it seems that the use of DRM systems to protect media content may be in decline. Since October 2007, DRM-free content can be downloaded for the same price as protected content from the Apple iTunes store. There are also several other online music stores that sell unprotected content. Also, by 2007, audio CDs from major music producers had ceased to use DRM. This probably happened not because of consumer anger, but more likely due to the large numbers of discs that had been returned as they would not play on various devices.

SAQ 5.2

You have now studied several different hardware and software systems or techniques for DRM. List the relative advantages and disadvantages of each of these approaches as you perceive them.

Answer to SAQ 5.2

Hardware approaches
Advantages: can be innovative; they are harder to overcome easily.

Disadvantages: may need to be compatible with older systems; can have a slow uptake in the market because they require new purchases; may drive potential customers to rivals whose systems are simpler or cheaper.

Software approaches
Advantages: can be innovative, they are more flexible so do not require the user to make an outlay on new hardware or formats.

Disadvantages: more easily overcome than hardware.

EXERCISE 5.2

DRM can be found in many consumer products such as DVD movies, HD-DVD and Blu-ray discs, video game discs and cartridges, eBooks, music downloaded from the internet and so on.

Spend no more than fifteen minutes looking for an example of such a product in your home or office. Try to discover from the packaging or any on-screen messages what restrictions are placed on your use of the product. You may need to use an internet search engine to discover more.

Do you believe these restrictions are fair? When you answer this question, try to consider both sides of the argument – not just the rights of the user, but also those of the content producer or the publisher.

5.4 Summary

There is the seemingly intractable problem that some people never want to pay for something that they can get for free. No matter how cheaply a shop sells a CD or DVD, it can never afford to give the disc away. Yet the internet allows people to obtain music for nothing. Thus some people will try to circumvent any protection scheme. Once the protection is broken, pirate copies will circulate. While it is not impossible that a foolproof system may be introduced, the likelihood is that piracy will continue, and the media and content producers can only hope to restrict its impact.

It has become something of a truism that any protection system can be cracked with sufficient time and resources. Generally speaking, the more valuable a commodity, the more effort will be spent on defeating any protection. This does not apply only to media products. All digital systems offer tempting targets, whether they are electronic voting systems, 'smart' identity cards or banking and credit cards.

Digital rights management seeks to control how users interact with data and is a technical solution to copyright infringement. In many cases it relies on users adopting new hardware or software. Both are susceptible to circumvention.

DRM can be unpopular with users if it constrains what they consider to be their legitimate use of a product (even though their perception of 'legitimate' may differ from that of the publisher). An unpopular DRM system will either drive potential customers into the hands of rivals, or encourage people to break the protection system (and the law!).

6 Privacy and access: a final word

Although this unit has concentrated on issues of protecting one's privacy, there can be advantages to having one's information available on the web. This section looks briefly at one example where publicly available information is generally viewed positively: in family history, genealogy and tracing lost family members.

Example 6.1   Finding the lost sister

A woman writing to the electronic magazine (e-zine) *Rootsweb Review* provided an example of how information can reunite people. An amateur genealogist and family historian, she posted her genealogical database on the web. However, she forgot one rule that genealogy websites generally insist on: living persons should be anonymous. Thus a living person appears on some of these websites only with the designation 'Living' followed by the surname. There is no birth date, place, current address or other information to identify them. This woman forgot to take out the information about living relatives when she uploaded her database.

Soon after, a man in Germany logged onto his computer at work. Every day for years he had done the same thing: enter a Google search for his lost sister's name. They had been separated in infancy, and all he knew of her was her adopted name and that she had been adopted in Florida. He had been trying to trace his sister for over 30 years, including employing a private detective. That morning, he was amazed to find the first response he had ever had to his enquiry. He quickly checked, and found that it was indeed his sister that appeared in the database: it even noted her original name before adoption and that she had a brother. Quickly he contacted the database's owner, who put him in touch with his sister, a relative of hers by marriage. His sister had also been searching fruitlessly for him, so it was with mutual joy that they were able to speak on the phone later that day.

That night, the database owner realised that if the sister's information was on the database, so was lots of other information about other living relatives, so she withdrew the database immediately in order to remove the information about living relatives. But in that brief 'window' between her uploading of the 'bad' database and its withdrawal, two people who had been searching for each other fruitlessly for decades were able to make contact.

Genealogical databases are not the only means of making contact, but genealogy using the burgeoning sources of information available on the web is a fast-growing popular hobby and has united many distant relatives. There are also websites concerned with finding former friends and acquaintances or members of organisations (such as the popular Friends Reunited website in the UK and Classmates.com in the USA). Other websites help people who were adopted or fostered to find information on their birth families (and sometimes to make contact). Families whose branches have lost contact with each other through emigration are now re-connecting using the web to trace distant members. With the information now available on genetic diseases, another use has been to trace members of families identified as having genetic diseases to enable members who may not be aware of the fact to be tested and possibly receive preventative advice or treatment.

The information available to searchers increases greatly from year to year. Information that was not available a year ago could be available next week. In many countries there are official (and unofficial) efforts to put indexes, extracts or copies of actual documents onto the web. In 2000, the US Government put the images of all the enumeration pages of the 1930 census on the web: it is now possible to view images of almost all the US censuses from 1790 to 1930. More and more of these are indexed so that it is possible to search by name rather than have to plod through pages of difficult-to-read documents. In the UK, the appearance of the indexed 1901 census on the web prompted hitherto unprecedented activity as people searched for relatives or amused themselves by finding out who had lived in their house all those years ago. Instead of travelling long distances to forbidding governmental offices, people can now use the web to browse computerised records from the comfort of their own homes. All English and Welsh census data from 1841 through 1901 are now available online. No more recent censuses are currently available because the UK's so-called '100 Year Rule' prevents publication of detailed census data within one century of its collection.

1901 Census

Many other countries are doing the same, depending upon what their laws allow. In Sweden, for example, the annual church censuses gathered for each parish since the eighteenth century are being indexed by dedicated amateurs, and images of the original documents made available on the web. Canada, however, resists releasing information in any of its censuses in this way; at best researchers may find another researcher who has compiled an index of some pages and posted this on the web.

EXERCISE 6.1

Can you see any problems concerning privacy in this explosion of information?

————————————— **Discussion** —————————————

I came up with two concerns. One is that a relative may be one of those best thought of as 'a skeleton in the cupboard': it is not everyone who would be happy finding that one of their great grandfathers had been in prison!

The other is a much more modern problem: identity theft. For example, a recent death could lead to an identity thief hunting out a birth certificate, a marriage certificate, or school or employment records, with the intention of pretending to be the dead person. The possibilities for fraud are obvious.

ACTIVITY 6.1

This activity invites you to think about tracking down other people. The links you can find are sometimes very surprising!

While information relating to families or genealogy within the UK is nowhere near as large as that available in the USA, you are unlikely not to find *anything*, and in some cases you may find (if you pursue this long enough) connections to others around the world.

I hope what you will gain from this section is a more personal view of the tensions that exist between a need for privacy and access to information, and that there are both advantages and drawbacks to hiding or making available such information. This brief example also raises the question of how much privacy (in terms of personal data about you that others had access to) people had in the past. The census and civil, professional and other records, including newspaper articles and notices, mean that people weren't as private in the past as we might have imagined. What has changed in the past decade or so is that, as sources of information such as past censuses and old newspapers are indexed and put online, modern modes of access to information about individuals have extended further and further into the past. The ease of finding such information has also increased dramatically. No more trawling through old archives for days on end – information is only a mouse click away, whether you want it or not.

7 Unit summary

This unit examined the nature of privacy and of surveillance, the tensions and contradictions that exist between making information publicly available and keeping it private, and the new tensions that currently exist between these because of technology.

Section 2 discussed the relationship between privacy and surveillance, and made the link between theories and modern technologies.

Section 3 examined spam and the hidden exchange of personal information through cookies. The Clipper chip encryption hardware, using key escrow as a means of allowing the authorities access when necessary, was described as a potential technical solution to protecting privacy that foundered through a combination of technical weaknesses and concerns about misuses.

Section 4 focused on the concept of intellectual property and copyright, and how digital technologies make it easy to reproduce materials in pirated form. It also looked at how a peer-to-peer network can evade control, and has the advantage of being very robust.

Section 5 described the response to piracy by commercial organisations – digital rights management. The tensions between purchasers' rights and copyholders' rights were discussed and some techniques for DRM were examined. The ongoing problems and flaws with any DRM system, given current technologies, were also explored.

The unit ended with a brief section showing how even the apparent privacy of the past has yielded to the open nature of the web, as old documents and census information is put online. Even the long dead can now be traced using the internet. If the implications for privacy are unsettling, it is well to remember that such an ability to trace people or institutions has also had the effect of uniting people. As with so much of technology, information made available freely and widely is a double-edged sword.

7.1   Learning outcomes

Having studied this unit, you should have achieved the following learning outcomes.

- Understand the concept of privacy and your attitude to issues surrounding it. (Activity 1.1)

- Understand the meaning and applications of surveillance. (Exercises 2.1, 2.2 and 2.3; Activity 2.1)

- State some of the costs of spam for the recipient and the internet service provider. (SAQ 3.1; Exercise 3.1; Activity 3.1)

- Define a cookie and describe how to find and control cookies on a computer. (SAQ 3.2; Exercise 3.2)

- Describe what a 'data flow' is and state how understanding data flows can be important to protecting one's privacy. (SAQ 3.3; Exercise 3.3)

- Describe briefly what key escrow is and state what the problems with such a technology are. (SAQ 3.4; Exercises 3.4, 3.5 and 3.6)

- Understand the importance of intellectual property rights and associated copyright issues. (SAQs 4.1, 4.2 and 4.3; Exercises 4.1, 4.2 and 4.3)

- Calculate storage requirements for the encoding of and time to transfer files over a network. (Exercises 4.4, 4.5, 4.6 and 4.7)

- Describe the need for compressing musical information before transmitting it over the internet and the differences between the two main techniques used. (SAQ 4.4)

- Explain how the Napster system for file sharing worked, and how it could fail. (SAQ 4.5)

- Explain briefly how a peer-to-peer network works. (SAQs 4.6, 4.7, 4.8; Exercises 4.8, 4.9)

- Describe some the possible conflicts between individuals and organisations made possible by encryption and peer-to-peer technology. (Exercises 4.10 and 4.11)

- Describe digital rights management and state the main points of the debate about it. (SAQ 5.1)

- Evaluate the impact of a technical solution on piracy. (SAQ 5.2; Exercises 5.1 and 5.2)

- List some advantages and disadvantages of different approaches to DRM. (SAQ 5.2)

- Describe the issues related to privacy with the online 'information explosion'. (Activity 6.1; Exercise 6.1)

Key terms 🔑

You should be able to define the following terms in your own words.

cookies	principle
copyright, copyright term	privacy
data mining	privacy policy
digital rights management (DRM)	public domain
digital watermark	ripper
escrow, escrow agency	robust watermark
ethics	sample rate
fair use	Secure Digital Music Initiative (SDMI)
family key	seed
file swapping/sharing	session key
fragile watermark	spam
in escrow	spam filter
intellectual property	surveillance
key escrow	time-to-live
key server	torrent
leecher	torrent file
Next-Generation Secure Computing Base (NGSCB)	tracker
	trade mark
patent	transaction
peer-to-peer	trusted third party
perceptual encoding	unit key
piracy	unsolicited commercial email (UCE)

References

Bentham, J. (1787) Extract from Letter I, Jeremy Bentham's *The Panopticon Writings*, Miran Bozovic, editor, London, Verso, 1995.

Deleuze, G. and Guattari, F. (1987) (trans. Brian Massumi) *A Thousand Plateaus: Capitalism and schizophrenia,* Vol. 2, Minneapolis, University of Minnesota Press.

Gowers, A. (2006) *Gowers Review of Intellectual Property,* HM Treasury, December, London, The Stationery Office. Available from http://www.hm-treasury.gov.uk./media/6/E/pbr06_gowers_report_755.pdf (accessed 19 May 2008).

ipoque GmbH (2007) ipoque Internet Survey 2007, *The Impact of P2P File Sharing, Voice over IP, Skype, Joost, Instant Messaging, One-Click Hosting and Media Streaming such as YouTube on the Internet*. Summary available from http://www.ipoque.com/news_&_events/internet_studies/ internet_study_2007 (accessed 19 May 2008).

McCahill, M. and Norris, C.A. (2002) *CCTV in Britain*, UrbanEye Working Paper No. 3 in the series 'On the Threshold to Urban Panopticon? Analysing the Employment of CCTV in European Cities and Assessing its Social and Political Impacts', Centre for Criminology and Criminal Justice, School of Comparative and Applied Social Sciences, University of Hull. Available from http://www.urbaneye.net/results/ue_wp3.pdf (accessed 19 May 2008).

Rose, F. (2002) 'The civil war inside Sony', *Wired Magazine*, November. Available from http://www.wired.com/wired/archive/11.02/sony.html (accessed 19 May 2008).

Stalder, F. (2002) 'Privacy-enhancing technologies and the voiding of privacy', Project seminar paper to the Surveillance Project, Queens University, Ontario, Canada (March).

Turow, J. (2003) *Americans and Online Privacy: The system is broken*, report from the Annenberg Public Policy Center of the University of Pennsylvania. Available as a pdf file from http://www.asc.upenn.edu/usr/ jturow/internet-privacy-report/36-page-turow-version-9.pdf (accessed 19 May 2008).

US Copyright Act 1976, Section 107, paragraph 1, reproduced online at http://www.law.cornell.edu/copyright/ copyright.act.chapt1b.html#17USC107 (accessed 19 May 2008).

Wright, T.W. (1998) 'Escaping the Panopticon: protecting data privacy in the information age', Georgia State University. Available from http:// web.archive.org/web/20040228190628/http://gsulaw.gsu.edu/lawand/ papers/su98/panopticon (accessed 10 March 2008).

Acknowledgements

Grateful acknowledgement is made to the following sources for permission to reproduce material within this product.

Figures

Figure 2.1: University College London Library;

Figure 5.1: MagicGate is a trade mark of the Sony Corporation, Japan.

Every effort has been made to contact copyright holders. If any have been inadvertently overlooked the publishers will be pleased to make the necessary arrangements at the first opportunity.